MW00676913

SPINNING THREADS

SPINNING THREADS

María Fernanda Suárez

NEW DEGREE PRESS

COPYRIGHT © 2021 MARÍA FERNANDA SUÁREZ

All rights reserved.

SPINNING THREADS

ISBN

978-1-63676-857-1   *Paperback*

978-1-63730-185-2   *Kindle Ebook*

978-1-63730-301-6   *Digital Ebook*

To all those who tell stories, and those who listen. Keep the threads spinning.

CONTENTS

NOTE FROM THE AUTHOR   11

PART 1   **17**
THREAD ONE   19
THREAD TWO   27
THREAD THREE   37
THREAD FOUR   43
THREAD FIVE   49
THREAD SIX   57
THREAD SEVEN   63
THREAD EIGHT   71
THREAD NINE   79

PART 2   **89**
THREAD TEN   91
THREAD ELEVEN   99
THREAD TWELVE   107
THREAD THIRTEEN   113
THREAD FOURTEEN   123
THREAD FIFTEEN   133
THREAD SIXTEEN   139
THREAD SEVENTEEN   145

PART 3   **153**

THREAD EIGHTEEN   155

THREAD NINETEEN   161

THREAD TWENTY   167

THREAD TWENTY-ONE   173

THREAD TWENTY-TWO   177

THREAD TWENTY-THREE   183

THREAD TWENTY-FOUR   191

THREAD TWENTY-FIVE   197

THREAD TWENTY-SIX   207

THREAD TWENTY-SEVEN   215

ACKNOWLEDGMENTS   221

NOTE FROM
THE AUTHOR

———

Dearest Readers,

For my great-grandpa, love meant following someone to the end of the world. Almost literally.

In 1947, my great-grandfather Luis met and fell in love with a young woman at a party in San Francisco. Originally from Costa Rica, Great-grandpa Luis came to San Francisco to study International Relations at Berkley. At the party, he couldn't help but notice a beautiful young woman with dark brown curls and shining brown eyes. She wore an elegant black dress and a gorgeous pearl necklace. When he approached her and they began talking, Luis learned Elza Vilella left her hometown of Rio de Janeiro to come study Art at Mills College.

As soon as the party was over, Luis started strategizing a way to run into Elza again. Standing in front of the school's billboard, Luis found the golden ticket to Elza's heart: a flyer requesting a chauffeur for Doña Berenice. He couldn't have missed that distinctive name anywhere; it was Elza's mom.

Although perhaps overqualified, Luis became Doña Bere's chauffeur. Driving the Vilella's up and down the streets of San Francisco, Luis became more and more convinced he'd found the love of his life. One day, when he showed up to pick the women up for a drive, he learned they had flown home to Brazil. The doorman at Doña Bere's apartment building couldn't tell him why they left so suddenly, but there had been talk of it being time for young Elza to go back home. For good. Luis decided it was now or never; he had to fly down to Rio and ask Elza to marry him. He jumped on a plane, determined not to lose the woman he loved.

A plane trip in the 1940s was an experience; it involved dressing up, an exclusive area with bunk beds where you could sleep, and a lot of wine. Aside from taking almost three times as long as flights do now, flights in the 1940s were also far more expensive. But most importantly, my great-grandpa Luis had no assurance he'd find the enchanting woman he was chasing. It wasn't as if he could text her to make sure he had the right address. He was taking a leap of faith.

When he got down to Brazil and tracked down Elza's house, Luis was told she and her mom had flown back out to New York to do some sight-seeing. Great-grandpa Luis was not about to give up; he hopped back onto another plane and flew to New York. As luck had it, by the time he got to New York and located the hotel where Elza and her mom were staying—going off the vague directions Elza's younger brother had given him—the two of them were gone, all the way back to Brazil. It was now about time for Luis to go back to San Francisco and finish his studies, but he was on a mission. He got on a plane, round 3.0, and flew to Brazil, committed to finding the love of his life.

And he did. Once he found her, he wasted no time: he proposed and married her in Rio to the tune of bossa nova and splashing waves.

As my grandma Cristina told this story to my twenty-one-year-old self, I was, needless to say, shocked. This type of out-of-this-world, romantic love was real? My great-grandpa had followed my great-grandma across borders and spent weeks chasing her, and all for what? The chance of talking to her? We all know they ended up together, but they didn't know they would at the time. The details of how well they knew each other before he flew out to find her were left out of the story I heard, but this willingness to travel the world for a simple *chance* at love touched me. There wasn't a "what-if-I-waste-my-time-for-nothing?" moment, or an "is-it-even-worth-skipping-work-for?" question lingering in the back of Great-grandpa Luis's mind.

My great-grandpa was certainly lucky he could financially afford to fly around the world looking for the woman he loved, but in today's world of cheap flights, I'm willing to bet the lack of affordability to follow love is more psychological than anything else. That's when I knew I wanted to pay tribute to this type of bigger-than-life love by writing what I, myself, love: fiction.

As the story I yearned to tell began taking shape, I wanted it to be a reminder of what should matter most: human connection. People nowadays believe younger generations are out of touch. Young people think old people have antiquated beliefs and can't understand modern concepts. Old people think the young ones don't care enough to listen to them. While there might be some truth to both sides of these beliefs, most of them stem from confirmation biases because we haven't bothered to hear the other side.

In a way, people from different generations are a mystery to us. I am, and have always been, a fan of mystery novels and TV shows, so I couldn't leave this mystery-loving side of myself out of my novel. While mysteries are fun and intriguing, I wanted the mystery I incorporated to serve as a reminder of the importance of understanding and coming to terms with our pasts. To tie it all together—because what is a story without love?—I also included some romance in my novel.

Today's fast-paced life gives us little time in between logging off our work computers and logging onto our personal ones to see social media, the news, the latest TV shows... We don't seem to have time for anything or anyone who does not bring us instant gratification in the form of professional advancement or social fulfillment. Through my novel, I want you to see how generational stories bring people together, helping them appreciate what really matters most in their lives.

It may be easy to write off someone as being too old or too young, but the stories of our elders are our past; the foundation upon which we've grown and become who we are now. On the other hand, the stories of the young are our present and our future. How can we really know ourselves if we turn a blind eye to either of these? I want you, as my readers, to be reminded generational stories not only create empathy for others but also help you, as a listener, learn more about yourself. My hope is this message is what you'll take away from my story!

Sincerely,
Maria F. Suarez

P.S. Aside from all these life lessons, I want you to be entertained by my story. So please have fun reading!

PART 1

THREAD ONE

———

I've heard all great stories are about love. And so, according to Juliana, it follows that all great loves are about stories. About living out these stories, yes, but even more importantly, about learning how to spin them.

Take a thread of yarn, cross it with another thread, and you have the story of two people. Cross it with ten thousand other threads and the story of these two people becomes more complete. One of these people is Juliana and the other... Well, since this is my story, I guess the other must be me, Penelope.

* * *

After graduating from college, I was eager to explore the world. As a romantic, I relished the idea of floating from place to place, experiencing all the world had to offer. My biggest concern, and the only thing truly stopping me, revolved around immigration paperwork and Visas. As an international student, I worked hard to get an OPT permission to work in the US for a year. Although I outwardly complained about this expiration date, there was some comfort in knowing nothing was permanent.

Like most romantics, I gravitated toward New York: the city of high buildings, high dreams, and even higher checks. And of course, I wanted to bring truths to light via the written word, which translated into me writing for a living at *Luxury Lifestyle Magazine* (Luxury L.S. for short).

Today, Silvy, Alice, and I decided to take a coffee break before our team's 4 p.m. planning meeting. We were all on the Editorial department's "Profile Piece" team, and we gathered once a month to discuss what the magazine's theme for these profiles would be. It was the team's February meeting, which meant each writer would be given the subject for our feature articles.

"Why are we always, like, weirdly color coordinated?" Alice wondered, as the three of us headed out to the Starbucks just down the street. She gestured with her ring-laden hands at the mint-green shirt beneath her coat, my green knitted sweater, and Silvy's olive-green cashmere frock.

Alice was my age, and we became great friends while interning at Luxury L.S. the previous summer. She was tall, skinny, and wore her long, brown-black hair down to her lower back. Like me, she graduated in December and had also just started working full time in January.

"I think people in the office think we plan this ahead of time," I offered, taking advantage of the break before the meeting to look at my Instagram. The outdoor air was cold on my exposed hands, and I quickly decided to forgo Instagram in favor of my fingers.

"Should we plan it once in a while just to mess with them?" Silvy asked. I had worked with Silvy on several feature pieces last summer, and she was awesome. She was a bit older than Alice and me, twenty-six now, I think, but she was super cool and stylish, so Alice and I liked hanging out with her.

"Yes!" Alice giggled, pushing the glass door open to allow us into the warm, coffee-scented air of a New York Starbucks in winter.

I ordered an almond milk small cappuccino. Once we all had our orders, Alice informed us we had exactly five minutes to sit and gulp down our coffee before we had to head back up to Luxury L.S. for the meeting.

"I'd like to propose a cheers," Silvy began, lifting her tall, black Americano in the air. "To these two superstars for joining us at Luxury L.S. I'm so excited to have you here again, guys!"

"Cheers!" Alice and I chirped, lightly tapping our cups—mine paper and hers a reusable plastic one with a golden Starbucks mermaid engraved on its side—to Silvy's.

"I'm so happy we both got offers to return after last summer. I really wanted to come back," Alice said.

"Same," I agreed, taking a sip of my cappuccino. I was happy to have had a job to go directly into after college. I had, after all, graduated a full semester early, and it seemed like I had a sort of head start on my friends and classmates. "Plus, I can't be too picky with my whole Visa situation, you know?"

"True." Silvy nodded. "How's that working out?"

"I got the one-year work permit, so all good for now."

"That's awesome." Silvy nodded.

"Now I just gotta prove myself as a writer to see if I get that sponsorship for a work Visa next year," I said, and after a quick pause, "but the odds of getting it are honestly kind of terrible."

"I'm sure you will." Alice smiled.

I hoped she was right because that was very much a big part of the plan: do well at my job, get a Visa sponsorship, work more, and figure out my next step. Something that would truly matter, I told myself.

"And if not, you can always marry Ricky," Alice added with a grin. Ah yes, my boyfriend, Ricky.

"I'm definitely not trying to get married this young, but worst case scenario..." I looked down at the dwindling stream of vapor that emanated from my cappuccino in waves.

Soon after, the three of us made our way back to Luxury L.S. and gathered, along with our team of six, on one side of the shiny, black-surfaced table in the Editorial conference room.

After a few people had been assigned their pieces, our boss, Adrienne, turned to me. "Penelope, let's see," Adrienne contemplated as her eyes scanned the piece of paper on the notepad she always clutched in her left arm. "You, oh, I know, this will be great. You're doing the piece on Luciano."

Sitting right across the table from Adrienne, I returned only a blank stare, after which she proceeded, "The painter. He did all of those abstract, modern paintings of people in forests that sold for millions. He's Italian but he also speaks some Spanish, so you'll be awesome for this."

"That sounds great!" I exclaimed, with the excitement and anticipation of someone who just got her first solo piece assignment. Alice had just been assigned her first solo piece too—one on a baseball player. I don't really care much about sports; and after having attended a single baseball game in my life about a year ago, I can confidently say it falls under the category of top most boring things I've endured. Following a painter for a month seemed ten thousand times better than that, so I considered myself lucky. Even if he was not as young and popular as that baseball player.

"It says here he's living in Naples, Florida," Adrienne continued, looking down at her pad again.

"Well, please don't come back with a horrible tan by the end of March," Alice joked.

"I promise I'll wear sunblock." I smiled back.

"At Pembroke," Adrienne declared, "that's the name of the condominium I think. I'll send you all the details later."

I nodded, my mind rushing in a million different directions as I thought of any college or high school friend who I could hang out with near Naples. My friend Kat, from a previous summer internship, was from Florida. But somewhere near Miami... As Adrienne moved on to assigning someone else a subject for their piece, I sneaked my phone out from my pocket and managed to type "distance from Miami to Naples, Florida" into Google, holding it right under the table.

"We'll find a long-stay hotel nearby for you," Adrienne said. "How does that sound, Penelope?"

At the sound of my name, I hid my phone beneath my thigh. "What did you say again?"

"I was saying that we'll put you up in one of those long-stay hotel rentals for a month or so, and you can go to Luciano's house in the mornings or afternoons and then come back to write. You can also get started on some research for other future pieces if you have extra time."

"Sounds good," I agreed, pretending to scribble something on the notepad that lay blank in front of me.

"Focus on capturing the 'that was then, this is now' sort of vibe around his brilliant career traveling the world when he was young and, well, where he's at now," Adrienne emphasized, waving the pen in her hand dramatically. "Being old and retired, I mean."

"Got it. That sounds great, really," I began, and saw an opening. "But you know what would be even better? If I could stay in the Miami area to get a more, um, varied and nuanced Florida experience, you know? It's just under a two-hour drive to Naples and I was thinking..."

"No, no, no, don't you go getting those ideas, Penelope. I want you near where he lives. You can go to Miami on the weekends." Adrienne rolled her bulging green eyes ever so slightly and moved on. She was nice, but I knew not to push her. Especially not on my first month at work and not when this job was the one thing standing between me working in the US or being forced to go back home. So that was that.

"Okay, guys. Focus on doing research for what's left of February. Come up with a proposal and an outline of what you'll be writing about in your Profile Piece. After that, I'll be sending you into the field to collect the information you need. I'm expecting these pieces by the end of March to come out for our April edition, okay?"

The six of us nodded in unison.

"Now go work!" Adrienne dismissed us with a wave. "Andy, you stay behind here for a moment. I want to talk to you."

Alice and I shot each other a half-surprised, half-concerned look of sympathy for skinny, shy Andy. Then came the awkward shuffling of papers as we all picked up our notepads and filed out of the meeting room, leaving Andy to his fate.

"So you wanna go for drinks after work?" Alice asked on our way back to our desks. "You might need them you know, before you devote yourself to joining the retirees down in Florida."

"Laugh all you want. At least I don't have to eat five hot dogs during each game to keep myself from dying of boredom," I retorted. "But yes, let's do drinks, please."

* * *

"What am I supposed to pack to interview an old man?" I asked into the rose-scented air of my room and waited for an answer from Ricky, whose voice materialized through the phone. On the FaceTime screen, I saw him floating on an inflatable lounge chair in the pool of his apartment complex near Duke. He was finishing college but not a semester early like I did, so we were long-distance. For now. The plan was once he graduated, he'd come to New York and I'd get the work Visa. Maybe.

It'd been a week since Adrienne told me I'd be moving to Naples, but I hadn't started packing until now; at 11 p.m. the night before my 8 a.m. flight. I took pride in not being a procrastinator with school, work, or chores... but weirdly enough, I always procrastinated packing. The only thing I had managed to actually put into my suitcase was the sheet-of-paper-sized painting of a row of traditional New Orleans houses, which I bought with my friends during one of our Fall Break trips to, you guessed it, New Orleans.

"I'm assuming you'll still need swimsuits. And shorts and shirts. Oh, and underwear." Ricky's deep, cheery voice rang through the phone.

"Of course, Ricky, but what shirts? Like, fancy and professional or casual and chill? And can I even wear *normal* shorts? Or do I have to buy those long-ass mom shorts? Definitely some going-out stuff for the weekends in Miami, but what about the stuff for every day?" I asked, piling most of the shirts, shorts, and dresses I owned into a heap on my bed.

"I... bro, what the fuck, I have my phone here!" I heard him howl to one of his *bros*.

"You what?" I asked, throwing a shirt with a little extra strength onto the pile, enough strength to make the whole pile crumble and fall to the floor. "Shit."

"Sorry, Loppy," Ricky replied, "the boys started throwing some water at me. They want me to go play soccer with them... They need one more, and they won't—"

"Go."

"Don't be mad."

"I'm not. Go."

"But you're being all—"

"I said it's fine."

"I'm sorry I didn't fly up there to help you pack and everything. I know I said I would but I have that exam next week and..."

And you have to lounge by the pool and play soccer with the bros, so there's no time to fly up here and visit me. I bit my tongue to keep the comment in. We'd had a few "fights" of this kind, and I wasn't about to get into it with all the packing I still had to do.

I settled for "Just go. You're not helping me here anyway. We'll talk later."

I hung up on him so I wouldn't have to see his droopy face, threw myself in the middle of the cloth pile, and, with a sigh, called my mom.

T-minus eight hours until I had to be packed up and ready to go to the land of retirees to live every twenty-something-year-old's dream.

THREAD TWO

———

I stood at the curbside of the Regional Southwest Airport in Ft. Meyers with a white beach hat on my head, holding a medium-sized suitcase in my left hand, and a big Longchamp handbag hanging from my shoulder. As I waited for the Uber I'd called to the extended-stay hotel Adrienne had put me in, I realized a strand of hair was stuck underneath the straps on my handbag. When I shifted to adjust it, my case-less sunglasses and my special pouch tumbled to the ground. I watched as cash, my grandma's bracelet, and a flash drive rolled onto the sidewalk. Great start. Picking up my fallen things, I started making a mental note to expense the Uber ride on Luxury L.S's account when a plain, silvery Nissan pulled up.

Half an hour later, I was dropped off at the hotel. There was no one in the dingy little lobby, and I had to say "hello" at least three times before an annoyed-looking woman with a messy ponytail came up to the front desk. We went through all the motions you'd expect, with her annoyance increasing when I didn't have a regular US ID and had to show my passport instead. Finally, she handed me the keys to room 323.

The first thing I realized when I stepped into my room was it smelled like cigarette smoke. I took a shower to wash the airport off me and stifled a cry moments later as I dried my hair and body with smoke-laden towels. *Just a month*, I reminded myself.

* * *

I woke up early the next morning, eager to leave the hotel and get started with my writing assignment. When I put the address to Luciano's house in my Uber, it read: Pembroke Retirement Community. So he lived in an old-people's home. Great. I requested the Uber nonetheless and convinced myself it wouldn't be as bad. Perhaps I could make some interesting observations about how my subject interacts with the other residents rather than just seeing him always alone?

Approximately eight minutes later, the Uber slowed down as he pulled up to a tall, black iron gate.

"You can drop me off here, I can figure it out," I said, gathering my handbag and my hat.

"You sure?" he asked, eyeing my wedges and the long road ahead you could see through the gate's iron bars.

"Yes," I replied, hopping out and ringing the bell on the intercom.

Behind the guardhouse at the foot of the gate, I saw a man pick up the phone and say, "Hello. Who's expecting you?"

"I... um, Luciano. I'm here to see Luciano."

"Last name?"

"Ríos. Well, that's mine. I don't quite remember his," I faltered, tying my hair up in a bun as I began feeling a few drops of sweat accumulating on my forehead. I silently cursed myself for not having studied Adrienne's notes on Luciano more.

"You're not on the list, ma'am."

"Can I just go in and talk to the supervisor? They'll know why I'm here. I just—"

"I can't let you in if you're not on the list, ma'am."

"Fine," I grunted, taking my finger off the intercom and fishing through my purse for my phone.

After two beeps, Adrienne picked up her phone. "Hey, how's—"

"He lives in a retirement community," I said, getting straight to the point.

"Oh."

"Yes, and I'm at the gate, trying to get in but they won't let me through. I need to be on a list, apparently."

There was silence for a few seconds, then: "I'll get you in. Give me a minute."

"Okay. Let me know as soon as I can go in."

"I'm on it," Adrienne said, hanging up and leaving me alone out in the Florida heat.

I walked toward a palm tree a few feet away and looked down at my white palazzo pants for a second before letting myself drop down against its trunk to sit under its spiky leaves' shade.

＊ ＊ ＊

After some fateful twenty-three minutes, during which I just scrolled aimlessly through Instagram, I got Adrienne's call.

"I got you on the list. I spoke with Lisa. She's the Marketing and PR coordinator at the community. Apparently, someone at Luxury L.S. wrote great stuff about Pembroke for a piece on the top retirement communities in the country a couple of years ago and that got them a bunch of customers. Anyway, she's happy to help. She'll be waiting to give you a tour, and they'll also let you in through the gate from now on."

"Great, thanks."

"Yes. Go kill it, Penelope, I know you can."

I hung up on Adrienne and rang the intercom's bell again. This time, the guard opened the gates and stepped out of the guardhouse.

"Ron's gone over to get the van to take you to the main building," he explained, gesturing toward the big structure at the end of the road. "Ron's our chauffeur," he clarified.

"That's not—actually, yes, thanks."

Within a minute, a white van with Pembroke's logo, two interlocked palm trees arching over each other, pulled up in front of me.

"Miss Penelope Ríos?" the van's driver, presumably Ron, asked, rolling down his window.

"That's me, yes," I replied, as he came out of the van and opened the passenger door. "Thank you."

He flashed a large, toothy smile, and we took off a minute later.

"So I hear you'll be coming to Pembroke over the next few weeks to talk to some of our residents."

"That's right," I answered absentmindedly, as I sent a text to my family group chat with my mom, my dad, and my sister Mariella in it. I texted Ricky separately.

"You'll love the place. It's great. So relaxing. And, this might sound hard to believe, but also fun."

"I did not expect the fun part." He was definitely not talking about the type of fun I was used to in college. Perhaps it was the cooking-and-piano-lesson, afternoon-tea type of fun. That I could believe.

"We have all sorts of exciting activities every day and the most interesting guests. Once," Ron lowered his voice and looked briefly to both sides, even though it was still just the two of us in the van, "we had someone from the Moroccan royalty come to visit a friend. And another time, one of the visitors turned out to be a criminal. Convicted of murder."

Now, this is what I needed to hear. Nothing like the thrill of royalty and crime to get an English Creative Writing major excited.

The van rolled down a wide road, split down the middle by a boulevard overflowing with blooming flowers; all pink, white, and yellow moving gently with the afternoon ocean breeze. A line of carefully plotted palm trees, arching ever so slightly, lined each side of the road. The majestic road came to an end at a rotunda, with a multi-layered fountain in the middle of it.

Ron pulled up to this rotunda with a proud smile. "We're here, Miss Penelope."

I stepped out to take in the building we had arrived at. It had a cream-colored stucco exterior with light blue wooden finishes around the windows that peaked out from the third, fourth, and fifth floors.

"Hello, hello!" A tiny blonde woman wearing a white skirt suit waved at me from the large wooden doors she had just opened. Lisa, I presumed. "We're so excited to have you visit us!"

"Thank you," I said to Ron with a nod and made my way to the entrance door.

"Hi, Penelope, it's so nice to meet you! I'm Lisa," the tiny blonde woman continued, offering her hand. "You're younger than I expected. And so pretty too!" she exclaimed, opening her mouth in a wide smile that exposed her extremely white teeth. For some reason, I had expected her to be older too. She seemed to be only in her mid-thirties.

"Nice to meet you too," I replied, returning her handshake. She was impressively strong for a woman her size. "Thanks for having me."

We stepped into the marble-floored foyer, which had a single, circular table in the middle of it. The table had a vase full of flowers, a stack of brochures, and a tray of glasses filled to the brim with some cold-looking liquid with drops of water condensing on its surface.

"You're so welcome! Now let me give you a little tour of our facilities. Before we begin, let me offer you one of our famous chilled lemonades."

"Thanks," I replied, grabbing one of the glasses and gulping down the drink.

"Great!" Lisa beamed. "So this building we're in now is the Pembroke Club House. We've got the main kitchen here, the formal and informal dining rooms, and this salon to our left where our guests can relax. They can also receive visitors here."

"It's beautiful." I observed as I took it all in.

The salon was all pastel-colored sofas, wooden-tied furniture, Persian rugs, and antique table-top decorations. I could immediately see why Pembroke was featured on Luxury L.S's list of top retirement communities. The walls were covered with pastoral decorative cloths of young boys and girls herding sheep in nature. There was a monumental piano sitting in one corner of the room and a few small tables scattered with board games on them. A few residents sat at the tables, but none of them bothered to look up at us.

The room made me feel like I'd stepped into the Château de Villandry in France, which I visited with Ricky last summer to see an art exhibit. He had waited for me outside in the gardens that day because he "couldn't bear the sight of one more Madonna and Child painting." Fair, I'd thought then.

"Upstairs, in this same building, you have the arts room, the library, and a gym. And then there are some resident apartments on the third, fourth, and fifth levels," Lisa continued. "You can explore all of that one of these days, but I want to take you outside. You'll love it."

Lisa directed me to the foyer again and down a hall that led to a pair of glass-panned doors, which she opened to let us out into the gardens. She was right; they were gorgeous. Several residents roamed the garden's winding sidewalks that cut through its bright patches of perfectly mowed green grass. I counted over ten couples of white-haired blobs walking hand-in-hand, stopping at the fountains and reaching out their hands to feel the tiny droplets on their skin as they splashed from one tier to the next.

Other residents walked with their arms locked around that of uniformed caretakers who stopped with them on the wooden bridges so they could look down at the water, lost in thought. It was almost ironic how all the beauty and exuberance of the clubhouse and the gardens contrasted with the residents themselves—indifferent looking at best, lost at worst.

A woman wearing a loose, white sundress with yellow sunflowers stamped all over it stood alone. She bent forward to cup a gardenia with both her hands and smell it. When Lisa and I walked past her, she looked up at us with hazel-green eyes and smiled. In the sunlight, her silver hair made her glimmer like a speck of reflective gold. A second later, she looked back down at her gardenia.

"Most of our residents live in one of these three other residential buildings," Lisa explained, gesturing toward the additional structures sprinkled throughout the gardens. They each have their own kitchens, gyms, and visiting rooms too. And then back there is our pool and the path to the ocean. It's a short walk out there but we have personnel to keep track of who leaves and when they come back. To make sure they're safe, you know?"

I nodded.

"I'm glad you like it. I knew you would!" Lisa beamed with pride. "We'll get to the important stuff in just a second. What you're really wondering is where to find Luciano, am I right?"

Luciano, that's right. Trying to figure out how I would stay sane for a month. Coming and going only from this place to my hotel almost made me forget why I was here to begin with.

"Yes, of course."

"He lives in The Palms building. This is a picture of him." Lisa pushed a small, passport-sized picture of a handsome man in his late sixties with gray hair and tan skin toward me. I figured the sharp angle of his jaw and his cheekbones should be enough to set him apart from the other residents. His dark brown eyes seemed to stare at me from the picture with profound intensity. He didn't want to be here, I guessed.

"Keep this picture so you can recognize him," Lisa continued, "You'll probably see him around. Most likely in the dining hall at The Palms. He also goes to the salon back in our main clubhouse a lot. He plays the piano there. Sometimes, although not as much as you'd think, he'll be in the arts room."

"Perfect," I said, jotting down a few notes on the notepad Lisa had given me.

"I could introduce you to him if you want. I wasn't sure how you guys—" *us journalists*, I was guessing, "work, so I didn't want to interfere with your interviews if you would rather him not know who you are."

"It's—"

"And he's not... how do I put this? He's not the biggest fan of the staff here, so you might have a better chance at cracking him if you don't get introduced by one of us."

"That works," I conceded, before Lisa started going on and on about the golf course's highest-quality grass.

Ideas on how to get the elusive Luciano to open up to me started darting through my head, bouncing off each other and drowning out Lisa's voice. I was not a fan of interviewees who spilled the very first second I spoke to them anyway. I always loved a challenge, so I figured I'd love Luciano; that is, once I found him.

THREAD THREE

——

I hadn't seen anyone who looked even similar to my subject when I collapsed into one of the pastel blue armchairs in Pembroke's clubhouse salon the following afternoon. Apart from the residents, there were about ten or twelve younger-looking people in the salon, which I presumed were visitors.

The heat outside was burning, and it seeped through the glass doors whenever they were opened in waves of hazy, heavy hot air. I remembered Lisa's instruction manual, which she handed to me at the end of our tour, and how it said you could ring a little bell at the entrance of the salon to ask one of the helpers to bring over water or snacks. I made my tired body stand up to ring said bell and, within minutes, I was gulping water dramatically. Perhaps a little too dramatically, because one of the residents addressed me in what I realized was the first real conversation I'd had with any of them aside from Curt's "hellos" and "excuse mes."

The resident was a short, plump woman with white roots racing to catch up with brown dye. She stopped her card game, with a girl I guessed was her granddaughter, and turned to me. "Are you alright, dear?"

"Yes, thank you. I'm just exhausted. From the heat," I clarified and managed to give her a polite smile.

"And who are you here for? This is my granddaughter, Kayla," she shared, grinning with pride. Kayla was probably a little younger than I, but I couldn't really tell her age on account of her heavy eyeliner and the sleek brown hair covering almost half her face. She wore a plain black shirt, dark jeans, and black Converse. I took her eyebrow raise and ever so slight nod as a hello.

"I'm not," I began, but changed my mind. I figured I could, perhaps, get some information from her on Luciano. Given I had no other leads on him, it was worth a shot. "...exactly sure where he's at. I'm here for Luciano. Do you know him?"

"Oh, yes, yes, he's wonderful! Kayla, you met him about a month ago, remember? He's the nice, handsome man who told us about the orchestra in Italy," the woman chattered.

"Mhm," Kayla replied, looking down at her phone. "Be right back," she added, excusing herself from the table.

"That's Luciano for you. He sure knows a lot about... art and music. Europe too," I offered, attempting to sound convincing.

"Once, a while ago, Remi's son was going to vacation in Florence and Luciano drew out a map for him with places to visit! Isn't that just marvelous? He knows so much. Did you say you're his..." the woman fished for an answer.

"Visitor, yes," I improvised. "I have to get going though. It was great meeting you, Miss..."

"Mary," she said with a warm smile.

"Mary, yes." I nodded, leaving the salon and darting into the bathroom.

As I entered, I heard someone inhaling deeply, followed by Kayla coming out of a stall and dabbing at her nose with a piece of toilet paper. Had I known more about drugs, I'd have been certain she was doing coke. On second thought, there's no way she wasn't.

"Don't judge," she spat, as she rinsed her hands in the sink. "At least I come to visit her. My other bitch cousins just take her money." She spun around and walked away.

* * *

I decided to do one last round through Pembroke's gardens to check for Luciano but to no avail. Hence, I was pretty defeated as I power-walked toward the gates to call my Uber and avoid being in the heat for any second longer than I had to. I was looking down at my phone, staring at the email that had just come in from Adrienne.

Subject: Update.

Body: Hey, Penelope, what do you have on Luciano so far?

I immediately flipped to my messages instead to find my conversation with Alice. I was going to complain to her about my assignment—and how Adrienne would absolutely kill me when she realized I had no clue where to start—when I nearly collided head-first with a woman. The gardens were empty at this hour because of the sun, but the woman did not seem to notice its burning rays. She wasn't wearing a hat or even sunglasses, so I could see her beautiful, green eyes, dotted with sparkling golden flecks.

"I'm sorry," I excused myself and stepped aside.

"I've seen you around here," the woman began before I had a chance to walk away. "What's your name?"

"Penelope." I tried to muster a smile but I wanted to be indoors, lying in bed and texting Alice.

"P-e-n-e-l-o-p-e," she said to no one in particular, holding each letter on her tongue for a few seconds, as if they were each a piece of chocolate she was savoring. "Penelope the weaver."

The gears of my brain churned quickly to produce an excuse that would get me out of this conversation. But I was too exhausted from the heat, so I just stared back at her blankly.

"Ah, don't tell me you don't know about her. She's your namesake! From Greek mythology, she was, what's his name? Odysseus! She was his wife." The old woman's green eyes sparkled fiercely through the folds of wrinkled skin that accumulated at the corner of each eye.

"That does sound vaguely familiar..." I reckoned, nodding my head as I recalled high school lessons on the literary figure of allusion. Allusions to Greek mythology, I remember discovering then, were everywhere. "I haven't read Greek mythology in years."

"Well, Penelope, as you might recall, Odysseus's Penelope is the emblem of fidelity. She kept on weaving that shroud for years to fend off the suitors who came to her. She would not give up. She was waiting for her husband to return from war. And she remained loyal until the day he returned to her."

"Didn't Odysseus have... didn't he cheat on her while he was away on his adventures?" I surprised myself by asking.

"Yes. Yes, he did." The sparks in the woman's eyes died down ever so slightly as she lowered her gaze. "Love is not perfect, Penelope. And I'm sure our Greek Penelope knew that. I'm sure she even knew what Odysseus was doing while he was away. But she promised to be with him forever. And she did just that."

"I'm guessing there was no option to get a divorce in those times," I added, momentarily unbothered by the drops of sweat starting to drip down my forehead.

"In Greek mythology, divorce is the least of punishments. She could have gotten her father, the King of Sparta, to kill Odysseus. She could have solicited a god to deliver divine punishment upon him. But Penelope understood what it was like to love unconditionally and that, let me tell you, is something your generation doesn't know."

It bothered me she was commending Penelope for taking her husband back after he cheated on her. It bothered me a lot she could never really know the truth of what he had done. I was about to get defensive, but I knew she annoyed me because she was right.

My generation would not stand for that shit. At the first sight of any discomfort in the horizon, we bolt. Better save ourselves before trying to pull up our partner so we can both stay afloat. But aren't we right to do so?

I nodded and excused myself. As I walked away, I realized I didn't even ask her name.

THREAD FOUR

———

I spent the next two days meticulously surveying each of the places Lisa had indicated I might find Luciano. No Luciano at the clubhouse salon, which was where I stationed myself for most of day three. I figured if he went up to the arts room or had any visitors, I'd see him there. But I didn't. No Luciano at The Palms dining room (and yes, the following day I sat in that dining room all day to make sure I wouldn't miss him). After a teary conversation with Alice at 7 p.m. on day five since my arrival at Naples, I resolved to cave and text ever-so-bubbly Lisa the next morning, asking for help locating my elusive subject. But when I woke up at 5:36 a.m. the following day, ready to text Lisa, I changed my mind.

It was a Saturday, and I still had one or two more weeks to go. Thankfully, Adrienne had given Alice and me some extra interview time given] this was our first solo assignment. Plus, I had ignored my friend Kat's text last night in favor of spending my Friday afternoon at a retirement community. My Friday night, I'd been wrapped up in smoky sheets. So I figured I deserved a break today.

A break will give me much-needed mental clarity, I reasoned with myself. Plus, I could spend the day catching up with my studies on art (I promised Adrienne I'd do some to enhance my piece and potentially write a follow-up piece on it), reviewing my outline for the Luciano story, and calling Mom and Ricky. *Have I really not called Ricky since that first day I got here?*

With these thoughts going through my head, I couldn't go back to sleep. It was still dark outside, but I sprang out of bed and made myself coffee on the portable machine I brought with me. My beautiful, extended-stay hotel room didn't have a balcony, but I slid open the window to drink my coffee with a luxury view of the parking lot. And that's when I heard it, very faintly in the background: the sound of crashing waves. The ocean. How could I have been in Florida for almost a week and not seen the ocean?

With a newfound sense of direction, I dove into my half-unpacked bag, changed into a black bikini, and pulled a red beach dress over it. I called an Uber as I slid my woven straw bag across my shoulder, fitting my phone and a light rolled-up sweater in it, before locking my apartment and walking off.

I set the destination to Pembroke and decided I'd just use its beach entrance. Pembroke was probably the last place I wanted to be on my break day, but the crime-obsessed side of me knew it was safer to be near someone when it was still dark out. And since I only knew Pembroke in Naples, then Pembroke it was.

The night guard was still on, but he let me through without any trouble. As I got closer to the beach, the sound of waves chasing onto one another endlessly on a futile race to reach the shore intensified. Unlike the air I had breathed ever since I got to Naples, the early morning air tickled my skin with a newfound freshness and saltiness I welcomed.

When I got to the beach entrance, I didn't see the personnel Lisa said were always there accounting for any residents who left Pembroke to make sure they came back, and the wooden-paneled gate was closed. Although not usually an adventurous soul, I was committed to getting to the beach, so I hoisted myself up the gate's lowest panel and prepared to fling my right foot over to the other side. As I did, the gate shifted slightly, revealing it had, in fact, been open. Note to self: check if gates are open before attempting to jump them.

The path to the beach was short and outlined by a pebble trail. Although it was still dark, I could see the stark contrast between the cloud-white of the sand and the deep blue of the water. I picked up my flip-flops in my hand when the pebble path came to an end to let my feet feel the sand below. I loved the feeling of it, cold and grainy, swallowing me into it. I felt so alive in the dark, with the wind and the water, that I let myself run a few yards along the water's edge, playing one of my favorite games as a child: run from the waves. My sister and I would run the length of our favorite beach in Costa Rica, the Puerto Viejo beach—our parents trailing behind as we tried to outrun the rising tide before giving up and splashing in it.

I was so focused on reliving my childhood game I didn't see the outline of two figures approaching me. When I finally looked up, they were only a few feet away. The sun was starting to come out, and I recognized one of the figures as the silver-haired, green-eyed woman who had spelled my name out loud and reminded me of its connection to Greek mythology. Instinctively, I started to turn around to avoid her, until I thought the figure next to her was... Could it be? There was barely any light, I couldn't be too sure. But what if it was him?

I stood still for a moment, thinking, before they caught up with me.

"Penelope, it's you, isn't it?" the woman asked, forcing her companion to stop too. I could get a better look at him now, and he had the characteristic angular jaw and intense brown eyes of the picture Lisa had given me. It had to be Luciano.

"Don't let us stop your jog!" The woman went on.

"No, don't worry. I was done jogging," I lied, catching my breath and managing a smile.

"This is my friend Luciano Savelli." The woman gestured to the tall, stern-faced painter. "And this is Penelope. She's recently been a frequent visitor at Pembroke but she never really told me why she's here." The woman tilted her head playfully in question.

Well, then. That was it for my cover, the one I wanted to keep to make Luciano more comfortable and have him open up. However, hearing his last name—which I had looked into ever since my initial failed attempt to enter Pembroke—confirmed he was, in fact, the Luciano I was looking for. I ran through my mental outline of what I had planned to say to him when we first met. I had a plan for this. *Think, Penelope.* Research, I was here doing research.

"Nice to meet your, sir. And you, ma'am, you said your name was…?"

"I hadn't said it to you before. It's Juliana," she said, the flecks of gold dancing in her eyes as the first rays of sunshine touched them.

"Juliana, yes. It's great to meet you. Officially, I mean." Neither of them offered their hand to shake. They didn't offer their cheeks either, as you would expect someone from Latin America to do, so I just stood there and smiled. "I came here to do some research. On Pembroke. The facilities and its residents. For a magazine." Technically not a lie.

"That's so interesting," Juliana mused, wrapping her arms around herself and rubbing at them with her hands. "Luciano here is sure to be a very fascinating subject for your research."

Right there and then, I decided I liked Juliana. My momentary doubts about her from our initial conversation evaporated slightly as she presented me with a golden opportunity to talk to Luciano without making him feel uncomfortable.

"I'm sure he is. Why do you say that exactly though?" I asked, trying to hide the excitement already building up in my voice.

"Why, don't you know who he is?"

"Juliana." Luciano spoke for the first time. His voice was raspy, guttural, powerful. It sounded like the very first burst of thunder at a distance; low but mighty. "It's okay. Why would this young girl know?"

"He's a famous painter!" Juliana couldn't contain herself.

"Wait... You're part of the Transavantgarde movement, right?" I was a bad actress, but I did my best to feign a moment of realization.

"Yes," they both answered in unison. Luciano's voice carried pleasant surprise in it, and Juliana's something more like satisfactory pride.

"I'm writing this other piece on European art of the twentieth century. I read about you, of course. I just didn't place you immediately." As I concocted this story, I wondered if it was the best avenue to get to Luciano. As part of our journalistic guidelines, I had to inform Luciano eventually I was writing a story about him. Maybe if I got him to warm up to me through his art, I could then tell him I wanted to give the story a spin and make it mostly about him. That sounded good.

"This is just meant to be! He knows so much—" Juliana began.

"Juli, please. Maybe the focus of... Penelope, right? Maybe the focus of Penelope's article is not my movement—"

"It really has no focus at all yet, Mr. Luciano," I interjected. "I'd be happy to learn anything from you. Truly, I'd be honored."

"Well, then, we'll set up a time to talk." Luciano nodded. "And no 'Mr.' please, just Luciano. I already feel old enough being here."

"That sounds great! When are you free?" I asked, perhaps a little too eagerly.

"Meet me on Monday at 8 a.m. in the arts room of the clubhouse. Does that work for you?"

"Yes, that's perfect." Honestly speaking, I would have agreed to an 11 p.m. or 4 a.m. meeting since getting access to him was the entire reason I was in this place.

"Let's head back now," Luciano decided and starting walking toward the path that led to Pembroke.

"He likes to go swimming before breakfast, when there's not too much sun," Juliana whispered to me as we fell back in sync, with Luciano walking a few feet ahead of us. "Plus, the guys who guard the beach entrance come out at 6:45. We have to get there before they notice we went out." As she said this, her eyes glowed like those of a mischievous child who was aware she'd broken the rules.

"The gate was open when I got here," I said out loud, without really knowing what I expected her to reply with.

Juliana produced a set of keys from the pocket of her flowy pants and jiggled them in the air.

"How did you—?"

"Let's just say one of the guards lost his keys in my hand a few years ago and vowed not to find them as long as I bring him the occasional lemon bars. I make them from scratch," Juliana said with a wink.

THREAD FIVE

———

"Do you mind if I sit here?" Juliana asked, looking at me from above and pointing to the spot in the sand next to me. It was Sunday, the day after she'd introduced me to Luciano, and I had come back to the beach again, this time in the late afternoon.

I looked up at her, feeling slightly annoyed. Couldn't she take a cue? I was holding a phone to my ear, for God's sake. Don't get me wrong, I was thankful to the woman for having introduced me to Luciano. That didn't mean I wanted to be her friend though. Something about our conversation on Greek mythology still bothered me, although I couldn't quite decide what it was.

"Hold on," I said into my phone and then to her, "No. I mean, I don't mind." I was speaking with Ricky, trying to tell him how Pembroke's gym didn't have the weights I liked and how I hadn't been able to go out to Miami to see any friends, but he was too focused on telling me something about a new challenge they were making their pledges do. I thought it was stupid.

If I excused myself to talk with Juliana now, I wouldn't have to tell Ricky the challenge was not only stupid but also pointless, and we wouldn't have to get into an argument about it. I also had to admit, even if something about Juliana bothered me, she also intrigued me.

"Oh, no, I don't want to bother—"

"I'll talk to you later," I declared into the phone and hung up. "I was done with that conversation either way," I said, digging my hands into the sand.

"Do you mind if I ask who it was?" Juliana opened her curious, green eyes wide to accompany her question.

I was not eager to share the details of my life or my relationship with her, but I figured I had to respond. "Ricky. My boyfriend."

"Ah, the boyfriend. I had a few of those before I ended up with Rob."

I nodded silently, looking out into the ocean. The faintest tints of yellow, orange, and pink had started dripping into the sky like a canvas, as if a watercolor painter had dipped her brush into the water and brought it back to the clean canvas, leaving behind traces of color.

"Do you want to hear the story about how I met my husband?" Juliana asked, almost timidly.

"Yes," I replied. Maybe if I got her talking about herself, she wouldn't keep on asking about my life. Plus, I doubted her life story could be worse than the stories I'd heard recently. As in, the story of a frat's challenge for its pledges. Now *that* was truly new and informative content.

"I was twenty and it was," she paused just a second, "1966. Oh, those were much better days before all the… Anyway, I was studying Classical Civilizations and Linguistics at, what's it called? At, um… Berkley! Up there in Northern California, you know?"

I nodded and offered a tight-lipped smile.

"Well, I'm from Brazil and I lived all my life there. I came from a family of politicians who traveled the world." Juliana gestured, drawing a circle with her hands. "My dad was in one of those famous UN conventions signing the Treaty of Peace with Japan. The 1951 one… Anyway, the world felt small, having lived all my life in Brazil. I was ready to leave. To travel. Explore."

Same.

I bit my lower lip as my mind started drifting to Ricky. He was smart and very passionate about his classes, even if what he studied was Finance. He even got involved in a startup and would light up with excitement when he talked about it. I loved that version of Ricky: sharp-witted and committed to succeed. But when he hung out with his frat brothers, a few of which I had in classes and who were actually super smart too, they all became boring. How many times would I have to hear the story about the time Josh, his pledge class's president, shot-gunned four beers back-to-back before throwing them all up in the pool?

Pulling myself from these thoughts, I realized Juliana was still going on.

"I was the oldest of five siblings, and my mom didn't want me to leave Brazil to study. She wanted me to stay home and help her and Dad host the receptions he held for politicians and their sons. She wanted me to find a suitable husband. And fast. She was a practical lady, that I'll give her. Maintaining five kids was probably not the easiest."

Of course, the story was funny. And I don't pretend to discuss the merits of Jane Austen or Mary Shelley every time we're at a party or hanging out, but maybe… I don't know. Just a little more insightful content.

"Thankfully, money was not an issue for her. But anyway, I was stubborn, and I wouldn't have it any other way than going out to the US to pursue my college degree… Are you hearing what I'm saying?"

I was still swimming in my own thoughts when I realized the constant hum of Juliana's voice had stopped. Shit. Did she ask me a question?

"What did you say again?" I tried.

"Have you listened to anything I've said?"

"Yes, I heard you're from Brazil but came to the US because…"

"Ah, I see, you've been hearing my voice, not *listening* to what I'm saying," Juliana replied, nodding pensively.

"There's a difference?"

"Hearing is passive. Listening requires attention. It's the actual processing of what's being heard."

"Interesting," I mused, genuinely interested in the semantic difference between the words. I didn't particularly appreciate being called out by a woman who invited herself to sit next to me and whose story I didn't ask to hear in the first place, but I was somewhat embarrassed to have been caught not paying attention.

"But you don't really care now, do you?" Juliana pressed on. The sun was about to plunge headfirst into the ocean and the painter's strokes had nearly all become shades of dark blue.

"About what?" I felt my stomach drop a bit.

"My story. Anything I have to say. I bet…" Juliana clicked her tongue and stared at me with a weirdly intense smile. "I bet you haven't talked to anyone here. Do you know any of the residents? You won't really make much progress with that article of yours if you don't actually listen to us."

"I mean, I did talk with Ms. Mary," I said, raking my brain for anything. Although I hated to admit it, the stubbornness in me wouldn't allow me to lose an argument. The only thing that came to mind was that interaction with the plump woman with white hair roots whose name miraculously came back to me now. That would do.

"Oh... And what did she say about her daughter? Is she back from that trip to Sweden yet?"

"I think... I think she mentioned her having just gotten back."

"She doesn't have a daughter." Juliana shook her head, but that shmuck smile of hers was still plastered on her face.

The initial annoyance that had briefly turned into embarrassment was quickly morphing into indignation.

"Well, maybe it was her granddaughter and I just—"

"You don't want to be bothered," Juliana interrupted me. "You don't want to have to deal with actually knowing our stories. Feeling our struggles."

I sat there, mute. Who did this woman think she was, to interrupt my phone call and start lecturing me about what I did and didn't want to do? What did she know?

"I mean, I don't blame you. You've had a good life. I've seen the clothes you wear and the handbags you carry." Her eyes, two green, fluorescent lasers in the darkness of the evening, scanned every bit of me. "And you're pretty. So really, why would you bother befriending the boring, old people here? Why would you care about their hardships?"

I still couldn't think of anything to say, so I pushed air out of my nostrils loudly to earn some time before I'd have to respond. The sun had taken its final dive into the ocean and the clouds had drifted away, leaving the sky an empty, dark blue pit of nothingness.

Something about Juliana made you want to tell her things. I can't explain exactly what it was. Even now, when I just wanted to push her into the ocean and not have to hear one more word from her, I wanted to explain myself. I think it has to do with the fact when she talks with you, she doesn't expect to be entertained. A lot of people either want me to tell them everything about my life, to keep them from thinking about theirs, or they want me to be the audience to their monologue and listen to everything about them. Juliana didn't seem to want either.

"Well, if you really want to know, I didn't come here to write about Pembroke residents or their stupid community. I couldn't care less about you all," I finally blurted with frustration.

"You came here to write a story on Luciano," Juliana replied, matter-of-factly.

"Was I that obvious?" I asked, momentarily forgetting I wanted to get out of this conversation.

"Who would remember Luciano out of all the European artists? No insult meant. He is a great painter, of course. But he isn't *that* famous."

"And do you think he...?"

"No. He has no clue. An artist's ego is way bigger than his sense of caution. I'm sure he didn't, not for one second, doubt he would be top of mind when someone thought of European artists."

"Good," I replied, staring into the dark water to avoid making extra eye contact with the woman.

Juliana shifted to her side, presumably preparing to stand up. After a brief balancing act, she hoisted herself up and looked down at me once before saying, "I didn't mean to be that harsh about what I said before. It's not all bad. My daughter is very much like you." Her eyes shifted and she stared out into the ocean before continuing, "And she's doing well for herself. At least, that's what I'd assume. We haven't talked in years."

With that, Juliana walked away, leaving me there, sitting alone in the middle of a dark, empty beach, digging my fingernails into the back of my thighs and resting my chin on my knees.

THREAD SIX

———

"Penelope!" I heard someone call at me from the clubhouse's salon as I was heading up the stairs to the gym. I recognized the voice after half a second: Juliana.

When I was on my way to work out, I disliked interruptions. But that was the last thought running through my mind at the moment. Juliana had shat on my character the night before, so much so I couldn't stomach the thought of dinner and I kept thinking about her words all night. Now she was calling for me? Why didn't she just leave me the fuck alone?

At the moment, I couldn't explain what drove me to spin on my heels and scan the salon for that woman, instead of just heading upstairs to the gym. I told myself it was because she was my only real connection to Luciano at the moment, and I couldn't afford screwing that up and getting kicked out of the job I fought so much for. It wasn't until afterward I admitted the other half of the truth to myself: Despite my best efforts to attribute her claims about my character to jealousy over my age, I knew she was at least partially right.

I stood at the entrance of the salon, searching the room for Juliana. I saw her sitting at a table with a man sitting across from her. The figure had his back toward me, so I couldn't tell anything about him. He didn't seem like another resident, though. I racked my brain to see if I could remember any male relatives or friends Juliana had mentioned during our conversation yesterday, but I could only remember her mentioning a daughter.

I didn't have to wonder for long, because as soon as I approached her table, Juliana said, "Penelope, I wanted you to meet my grandson, Peter. Peter, meet my," she paused a second here, "friend, Penelope."

"Nice to meet you," the grandson, Peter, replied, slowly turning his head to see me.

The first thing that struck me about Peter were his eyes. They were light brown, the color of burnt sugar, outlined by long, black lashes. And they sparkled the same way Juliana's did. He had a warm, wide smile with bright white teeth. Perhaps a little too perfect of a smile. His hair was brown and neatly trimmed, but not too short. He wore a simple blue button-down shirt and khaki pants. It was refreshing to see a guy around my age not wearing sweatpants or an old t-shirt, like they all did in college. Like Ricky did. Always.

"Nice to meet you too," I replied, suddenly feeling self-conscious of the fact I was in the exercise clothes I had used yesterday and was wearing my hair up in a disheveled bun. "I... Juliana hadn't mentioned she had a grandson."

"Well, thanks, Grandma, I can see how much I mean to you," Peter joked, glancing at his grandma and pretending to be hurt.

"That is not true at all!" Juliana protested. "I must have mentioned him yesterday when we talked about... I guess I didn't tell you much about my son either," she finished, her voice becoming quieter at the end of the sentence as she looked down at her hands, interlaced on the table in front of her.

"I probably just forgot," I offered, mostly to avoid the awkward silence I was sure would ensue after her comment but also because I felt the slightest pang of guilt building up when seeing how upset she suddenly seemed.

"And I'm kidding, Grandma," Peter added, giving her one of his perfect, warm smiles. "Would you mind telling me what it is exactly you're doing here?" He shifted in his chair to face me again. "Grandma tells me you've been coming over to Pembroke for the past few days, but she hasn't told me exactly what made you come here in the first place... Aside from the beautiful gardens, of course."

"Wow, you got me there, it was the gardens." I was not one to engage with jokes much, but I appreciated how he had brought it up in a way that wasn't annoying.

After giving Peter a quick spiel about my job at Luxury L.S. and my piece on the community at Pembroke and the other one supposedly about European Art, I excused myself to go to the gym, Peter's face still floating in and out of my thoughts as I ran on the machine.

* * *

I jogged down the stairs of Pembroke's clubhouse, feeling energized after finishing my workout. I'd been exchanging funny memes with my sister Mariella and finally managed to get Peter's face out of my mind. That is, until I saw him push open the clubhouse's main door and rush in, a drop of sweat racing down his forehead.

I was going to pretend I didn't recognize him and walk away, but he stopped me.

"Penelope! Sorry to bother you."

I was red from running and sweating profusely. I really didn't want to be speaking to him when I looked like this. *But what does it matter? It really shouldn't matter at all if he thinks you're ugly.*

"Yes, what's up?" I wiped my face with my towel, but I felt a thin layer of sweat starting to build over my lips almost immediately after I wiped it away.

"Would you do me a favor? The guard at the entrance... He's not there. I'm not sure why. I can get the gate to open, but someone has to hold it so the car can go through. Otherwise, it just starts closing when you let it go…"

"And I'm guessing I'm the chosen gate-holder?" I hated I couldn't help myself from letting that playful tone come out with him. That playful and, some could say, almost flirty tone.

"Would you do me the honor?" he asked, with a perfect smile.

"Sure."

We started walking in the Florida heat toward the exit. I knew the walk to the gate was a few minutes long. Just as I began to wonder if we would walk in silence, Peter said, "If you don't mind me asking, how old are you?"

"Why would I mind?" I asked back, wrapping my exercise towel in a tight loop around my hand.

"I don't know. Some girls really dislike it. I always guess too young or too old."

"If you had said twenty-two, you'd have been just right."

"That's around what I figured. Those were some good years," he added, looking up into the cloudless baby blue sky.

"You can't be that much older yourself."

"Only a full five years."

"That's not too bad."

"I guess it isn't." His smile faded, and he was suddenly quiet.

In the spirit of avoiding awkward silences, I went over to the gate and began pulling it open. When he still hadn't said a word for what seemed like more than a minute, I began wracking my brain, thinking about what to say next. Thankfully, he spoke first.

"Thanks for getting the gate. Otherwise, I would've had to move in with Grandma and I'm not sure they're taking residents under the age of thirty yet."

"Maybe they'll save the first spot for you," I said, my hands still on the gate. Peter, who'd been fumbling around his pockets for his keys, now stood there in front of me, keys in hand.

"I just have to say," he paused again, "I really like your accent." I felt my cheeks grow warm, and I was sure they were turning red. Hopefully, it was masked by my just having exercised and the afternoon sun. For the first time today, I was glad I looked like I had exercised. "Is it bad of me to point that out? Is it offensive?" he asked, suddenly concerned.

"No, no. At least, I don't think so," I reckoned.

"So where are you from?"

"Guess." Again, I hated myself for being playful.

"Let's see... Could be somewhere like... Colombia?"

"Not quite."

"Or more like Ukraine?"

"No, not at all! Colombia was much closer. Think Latin America." For some odd reason, people often thought my accent was Eastern European.

"Spain?"

"Think Central America."

"Oh... Guatemala?"

"Costa Rica," I said, giving in.

"I've heard it's beautiful. The beaches, the mountains, the people…"

"You'll have to go and see for yourself."

"You just proved they were right. About the people at least." With that, Peter hopped into the front seat of his red Jeep Cherokee and shut the door.

I turned, so he wouldn't see my cheeks grow even redder and kept a hand on the gate, holding it open until his car zoomed past it.

THREAD SEVEN

———

I spent the rest of Sunday afternoon reading up on European art to make sure I'd be ready for tomorrow's meeting with Luciano. My first feature article had to be perfect. I called my sister to get her help on brainstorming questions I could ask to get the most interesting information out of this man. She was brilliant and, although we didn't call each other super often, I knew I could always count on her for help. I didn't, however, tell her about my conversations with Juliana and her grandson Peter. I didn't tell anyone.

I think I didn't mention these conversations because I had absolutely no idea what to make of them myself. I hated that Juliana's comments bothered me. I do care about people. She didn't know me at all, so why did she think she could go about making these claims without knowing? But then again, do I *really* care? Or do I only care when it doesn't inconvenience me? Once I steered my thoughts away from Juliana, they collided headfirst with Peter's smile. His beautiful smile. It took a while before my mind could fully settle on art.

* * *

On Monday morning, I sprung out of bed with the unyielding energy of someone committed to writing the best feature piece, one that screamed *"you are a great writer, even if English is your second language!"* and *"we would totally want to sponsor you to work with us after your student work permit is over!"* I drank my coffee, staring at the extended-stay hotel's empty parking lot to clear my thoughts and focus on reviewing my notes for the upcoming interview.

After putting on a simple pair of jeans and a short-sleeved button-down shirt, I hopped in an Uber and made it to Pembroke's clubhouse in under twenty minutes. Remembering Lisa's layout instructions, I made my way into the arts room, took a seat at one of the round tables, and tapped my foot on the ground as I waited for Luciano. After a few minutes of sitting alone, I started worrying. Did he forget? Had we agreed to meet at seven instead of 8 a.m.? Was I a full hour late? I checked my phone again and the time read "8:08 a.m." He's Italian, I reminded myself. He's also old; he's allowed to be late.

At 8:12 a.m., Luciano strode into the arts room, holding a mug in his left hand and a phone in his right one. He took the room in slowly, as if he had not been here before, or as if there were much to look at—either of which was most definitely untrue—and finally settled his gaze on me.

"Penelope, let's get to work." He positioned himself on a stool in front of a blank canvas and set the mug and his phone down on a long three-legged side table, picking up the paint palette that was on the same table.

"Hi, Mr. Luciano, I think you... I don't paint. I *write* about art. I don't create it," I clarified, growing somewhat flustered.

"You couldn't have said a more incorrect statement," Luciano countered, his voice soft and soothing like a cup of mint tea. "Writing is art too. Now come on, take a seat next to me and just start putting your brush to the canvas. I'm not asking you to create a masterpiece yet." He winked one of his penetrating brown eyes subtly and went back to mixing colors.

I scanned the room myself for the first time. Along the right wall, a line of stools faced a matching set of easels. A set of enormous windows made up the back wall, and the room glowed with the sun's warm touch. Every easel held a white canvas, and next to each mini station was a side table with oil paints. On the left side of the room was a drying station where artworks were left to dry. There were also several big, round tables, presumably for collaborative art or social breaks. I was sitting at one of those tables, looking at Luciano's back as he began covering his canvas with delicate, turquoise strokes.

I was not going to get him to talk with his back toward me, so I took a seat on the stool next to him and plunged my paintbrush into a blob of blue paint.

"So Mr. Luciano, I take it you're a Transavantgarde-ist," I tried.

"In art, you could be everything and nothing at the same time," he replied, eyes set on his canvas. "You can be a Romanticist without the natural elements. Which means you could say you are an Expressionist. So I don't say I am one thing or the other. But, to your question, I guess you could say I am."

"Okay, okay," I said, looking down at my notepad to read off the next question, while still awkwardly holding my paintbrush to the canvas. "When you sit down in front of a blank canvas, what is your first thought? Do you plan what you'll be drawing ahead of time or do you just… improvise when you sit down?"

"It can happen either way. One of my favorite paintings, *La Signora Nella Foresta*, I began and nearly finished in one sitting. And I didn't plan it at all. I started off drawing a naked woman. She was naked and alone. I felt her fear; being so exposed and so isolated. Then I drew trees around her. Suddenly, there were branches braided in her hair and she was in a forest."

He *felt* the fear of a naked and alone woman. *Of course, he did.* "That's great," I said, recalling the *La Signora Nella Foresta* picture I'd seen in Google when I looked up Luciano earlier that morning.

"Thank you." Luciano beamed, twirling his brush in loops to create some abstract-looking foliage. "I was twenty-three when I painted that. Newly married. My wife Marietta was away on a trip with her older brother because he was sick, and she didn't know if he'd live through the Florentine winter. She took him to a beach by Livorno… Anyway, you're writing about the art movements in Europe, right? And here I am boring you with my life story…"

Shit. He was doing exactly what I wanted him to do. But not what I told him I wanted him to do. Damn it.

"No, no. I'm very interested in your story actually," I said, going with a bit of pointillism to add texture to my plain blue strokes. It could become an ocean. Or a sky. I had no clue what I was painting and was sort of waiting for the painting to reveal itself to me.

"You are?" Luciano's eyes lit up, but he still didn't look away from his canvas.

There was that artist ego Juliana talked about. "I was thinking, maybe, I could focus my piece a little more on you, if that's okay," I ventured. "Instead of doing it on all the art movements in general. It would make it much more interesting for our readers, you know?"

Luciano let the words hang in the air unanswered for what seemed like a few minutes but was really only a fraction of one. He finished the neat outline of a leaf and set his brush down to look at me. I hadn't made much progress on the blue wavy then dotty lines that were to become an ocean or a sky, but when I met his laser-digging eyes, I picked up my brush again and started filling my canvas with more blue to avoid holding that all-engulfing gaze.

"Well… if you think it's better for the article, then yes. My life is not interesting and adventurous like that of… of Van Gogh, but…"

"Oh, that's no concern. Readers like relatable artists. And I'm sure your life is very interesting. You're from Italy and now you're here, there's a story there."

And what a quintessentially romantic story it was.

Luciano was one of three sons and two daughters of a baker in Verino, Italy. He and his siblings would do door-to-door bread deliveries. But they also had a lot of free time; to run around in the town's woodlands, getting lost in between the spruces, oaks, and beeches, and coming back home with their pants ragged and their knees covered in mud. That's how he developed his love for nature.

As for art, he developed his love for painting because of a girl.

Marina's house was a forty-five-minute walk from Luciano's, but he always volunteered to deliver bread for her. Marina had two younger sisters, both of which were infatuated by the well-built, beautiful-eyed son of the baker. But Luciano only had eyes for Marina, who was probably well over ten years older than he.

She was usually sitting on a stool in front of a canvas, moving her brush in ways Luciano had never seen an instrument move before, and bringing pictures of the wildest things to life.

She created women's faces and women's bodies out of a few brush strokes. She made them happy or sad at her will. When she drew, Luciano saw a fire burning in her black eyes. It was a furious fire that burned with all the passion in the world and would stop at nothing. Luciano would stand, staring at her and her art, for as long as he could before Marina's mother or father would suggest it was time for him to go home. But when her parents were away, Marina would give Luciano a canvas of his own. That's when he began painting.

Luciano stopped going over to Marina's when word reached him that she was to be married to the son of the town's architect. At fourteen, he went over one last time to internalize the fact that this was the end of seeing Marina, of watching her create beautiful art, and of painting. But when he came over that day, Marina was not sitting in front of her canvas. She was sitting with her back against the wall, her elbows resting on her knees, her hands holding her head, and her golden locks spilling down, brushing the floor. When she lifted her head to look at him, Luciano noticed that something in her eyes had changed. The fire; it was gone. And so were her stool and easel.

Luciano knelt in front of her and asked what was wrong. He peered into her eyes, trying to see the spark that he knew was still in them. When she finally looked him straight in the eye, he saw some of it.

"Don't let anyone take art away from you. Any-one, you hear me?" Marina said, breathlessly. Then she grabbed Luciano's face in her hands, pulled him over, kissed him, a hard and passionate kiss, and then let him go. That was the last time he ever saw her. It was also the start of his art career. He bought some canvases for himself and never let anyone stop him.

After wrapping up this story about how he got into art, Luciano suddenly asked, "Why is it that you're here? At Pembroke, I mean?" He tilted his head pensively.

"Just, general research. I'm... I'm writing another article on the sense of community in retirement homes." I can proudly say I've never been a good liar on the spot, but that came out pretty well.

"Oh. Okay. And how long are you staying in the area?"

"A week or two more."

"That's perfect. What do you say we meet once or twice this week and the following one to work on our art, and I tell you a bit more about my work and my life?"

"That would be great. I'd love that. So we would meet...?"

"I'll let you know when I'm inspired and come up here. I don't exactly paint every day. It's more when the inspiration hits. A few times a week usually."

"Yes, of course. So how exactly would I know when—"

"You do realize I am seventy-nine, not 109. I can text you." Luciano chuckled, handing me his phone with the 'new contact' page brought up so I could put in my information.

Just as I saved my number in his phone, my own began ringing loudly from inside the pocket in my jeans. I took a quick look at it. Ricky.

"Do you need to get that?" Luciano asked, trying to peer at the name on the screen.

"No," I found myself saying all too quickly. "It's not important." It probably was. Or not. I just couldn't bring myself to wonder why I answered like I did so quickly.

THREAD EIGHT

———

"Dear residents, staff, and visitors, we have an important announcement to make," said a vaguely familiar voice that seemed to come from everywhere and nowhere at the same time. "Starting tomorrow, the Pembroke Residential Community will begin preparations for the rapidly-approaching Category-3 hurricane."

It had been a pretty uneventful Tuesday afternoon until then, and I had just been walking through the gardens to pass time. I'd read all there was to read about Transavantgarde art and since I could not really do much more for my Luciano story, except wait for him to feed me information, I decided to go on a walk. I was prompting myself to call Ricky, but the afternoon was so nice and sunny, so calm and quiet… That is, until the voice I now recognized as ever-so-perky-Lisa started booming through the invisible loudspeakers that were apparently hidden in every corner of the gardens.

"Due to the potentially devastating effects of this hurricane," Lisa continued, presumably reading off a script, "all residents are to remain on alert as we track its path and make preparations for a potential evacuation. Residents' mobility in and out of Pembroke will be limited strictly to emergency medical visits. To streamline the evacuation process, in the case one becomes necessary, no visitors will be allowed in our facilities until further notice."

During the whole week I'd been in Florida visiting Pembroke, I had not heard a single announcement over the loudspeakers. I had also not really thought about the approaching hurricane yet either. I knew things were starting to get bad in some Caribbean islands, but the US? I thought we were doing just fine. I sat on the border of one of the fountains, somewhat taken aback, and looked around to see if the residents were as baffled as I was.

"If you have any questions or comments about these guidelines, please call or email me. You can also find me at the clubhouse's main office on the second floor from nine to five."

For a minute, before everything set in, I just sat there and looked around.

A couple, both of them probably over eighty-five, seemed completely indifferent about the announcement. They continued staring at the water in the fountain, mesmerized by its incessant flow. Despite how loud the announcement was, I wondered if they heard it at all.

A nurse walked by, holding an old man by the arm. He was asking her what they had just said as she, notably pissed, let go of his hand, pulled out her phone from her pocket, and started screaming at someone on the other end.

Then, I noticed a woman wearing a loose lavender dress that came all the way down to her ankles. Her powder-white hair was tied up in a neat braid, and she was sitting alone at one of the tables, tears streaming down her face.

I wanted to call my mom. I wanted to call Adrienne and tell her I was giving up on this assignment because of the hurricane and would fly back to New York. But for some reason, before doing so, I decided to approach the woman in the lavender dress and pull a chair to sit next to her. *See Juliana? I can be nice.*

"Hi, my name's Penelope. Are you okay?" I asked, trying to make myself sound comforting.

"I," the woman said, gasping for air as she sobbed, "I'm... what was I saying, dear?" She stared at me innocently with big, round eyes and a soft smile.

"You... um... I was asking if you were okay," I repeated, unsure what to do about her sudden mood change.

"Why, I don't know. I think I am. Where's Mom? She'll tell you."

I heard the fountain's water pounding, flowing from tear to tear, and I reminded myself why I always avoided speaking to the residents in the first place: one, there was not much to say and two, most of them could either not hear well, remember well, or both.

"Yes, I'll ask her." I smiled. "What's your name?"

"I... I don't know," the woman said, shifting a little uncomfortably in her chair.

I was about to excuse myself when an old man in a well-ironed shirt approached us.

"There you are, Annie," he said, rubbing the woman's shoulder as he bent down to kiss her on the cheek. "Did you just hear what they said?"

"Yes," Annie replied, nodding somberly. "Mom won't be happy."

The man shook his head and sighed before he seemed to notice me. "And who are you?" he asked.

"Penelope. Excuse me," I began getting up from the table.

"There's no need to leave, Penelope, you can stay here. I'm sorry if Annie sat in front of you without asking. You see, she's having some trouble remembering to ask..."

"Please, don't worry. She was here first. I saw her crying and came over to ask if she was okay. But she didn't seem to remember why she was crying," I explained.

"Oh. Maybe the news upset her. Or maybe it was just the loudness of those speakers. They almost gave *me* a heart attack," the man joked. "I'm Donald, by the way," he added, offering a hand.

"Nice to meet you." I shook his feeble hand. "I do have to get going though. But it was nice meeting you both."

* * *

I walked a few feet away from the couple before calling Adrienne. Thankfully, she picked up almost immediately. "Any progress?"

"Actually, yes. I had my first interview with Luciano, and I got him to give me the whole story of how he got into painting. It's quintessentially Italian and romantic. But that doesn't matter, because I have to fly back out to New York tonight."

"What do you mean?" Adrienne's voice was flat.

"The retirement community is going into a sort of lockdown. Because of the hurricane that's coming, you know? So they're not allowing visitors in anymore."

"So we get you a room in the community," Adrienne replied, as if that were the very obvious, logical thing to do. "They always have a few unoccupied ones, and I doubt any new residents will be moving in during a hurricane."

"No. What do you mean? It's a potentially devastating hurricane, Adrienne, I have to get out!" I stood up from my seat at the edge of the fountain and began pacing.

"Penelope, if those old people will be fine, I'm sure you'll be fine too." I could almost picture her rolling her bulging, reptile-like eyes at me.

"But I already met my subject, so I could call him from—"

"No 'buts,' Penelope. How many award-winning pieces have you seen cite a *phone conversation* as their main source? How many have described the way a subject picked up the phone versus how they walked with a limp? How they looked longingly at the kids walking by for a second too long?"

None, I thought, but said nothing for what was probably a second too long for Adrienne.

"Look, I know it's not ideal." She cut through my silence. "But you're strong. I know you can handle it. I could always get you off this piece and have you wait until the next cycle to—"

"No." I jumped at that. If I had no assignment to do for months, I'd for sure be fired, and that meant bye-bye Visa. "I can handle it."

"Now that's the spirit." I could hear her typing and scribbling in the background. "I'm calling that woman from the community—what's her name?—to get you settled there."

"Lisa," I said, staring off into the direction of the ocean. The gardens had emptied out and a dark gray cloud settled over the horizon.

"Yes, Lisa. I'll call you back once everything's settled."

* * *

After an hour, during which I mostly just alternated between staring off into space and staring down at my phone—unable to bring myself to tell my mom or Ricky about the hurricane yet—Adrienne called to say Lisa was ready for me at the clubhouse, so I had made my way back there. Adrienne was right; there were a few empty rooms, and they'd be giving me one.

As I walked in, Lisa was coming out of her office. A gravity-defiant strand of hair had broken loose from her tight bun and was sticking out to the side. She walked as quickly as her tiny steps would allow her to until she met me.

"We're so excited to have you staying with us here at Pembroke for a bit," she squeaked, handing me a folder with the words *Welcome Packet* written across it. She didn't stop and rather kept walking toward the glass doors that led to the gardens. I trailed behind.

"So you already know the place. You know where everything's at, right?" It was not so much a question as a statement.

"Yes."

"Great. Just let me show you to your room. It's one of the ones that's vacant now."

We walked into the residential building called The Palms and took the elevator to the fifth floor. Lisa pulled a key card out of her suit's pocket—today her suit was all gray—and directed me to Room 506. I noticed my bags were already waiting outside the door. Adrienne had apparently arranged for Ron, the chauffeur, to go pick everything up from my hotel room. Although it was troubling to think Ron had to go through my unpacked stuff when I could have perfectly done it myself, I was glad I didn't have to return to that stinking hole. Plus, I was carrying the most important things—my passport, my laptop, and my pouch—in my handbag.

The apartment itself was simple and clean, with a minimum amount of furniture and décor. But I immediately noticed it had a breathtaking view of the ocean from the balcony.

"I'll give you some time to get settled. Then meet me back over at the clubhouse and I'll take you to dinner. Sound good?"

"Yes," I said, and it sort of did.

A few hours later, I found myself sitting cross-legged in a spacious dining hall, staring intently at my phone to avoid thinking about how hungry I was. I'm a big snacker, and I had finished the granola bar and gummy fruit pack I brought with me to Pembroke. Note to self: go out tomorrow and buy snacks. Could I even do that though?

Most of the residents around me sat in silence, consumed entirely by the task of eating each bite of smashed potatoes and cod. I briefly considered striking up a conversation with an old man who was wearing a CSI shirt, but the truth is I feared conversations with frequent awkward pauses when I had no escape plan. Awkward conversations were basically my job, but if I were following a politician around his office, one of us would always have somewhere to go. That was clearly not the case here, so I chose to sit in silence and scan the room. Observation is a form of primary research after all.

I opened up Lisa's welcome package where she had written pages full of notes in her perfectly round calligraphy, detailing several aspects of Pembroke. Under the *Dining* heading, I saw some time frames and locations. Dinner ended at seven. I winced a little. Dinner at home didn't *start* any time before seven.

Finally, Lisa strode into the dining hall. I noticed she'd fixed her bun.

"Hi, how's it going?" She paused only for a second and, before I could respond, resumed speaking. "So early each day, you get a paper menu with fill-in-the-boxes squares saying what will be available for lunch, dinner, and an afternoon snack. It usually gives you two options. Such as chicken or fish with pasta alfredo or mashed potatoes. So you select what you want and bring the menu with you to the dining room at breakfast. I picked the pasta alfredo and chicken for you today but I forgot to ask, do you have any allergies or dietary restrictions?"

"No, I don't." Except for, maybe, I don't want to be two hundred pounds when I leave this place.

"Let's go get the food and I'll walk you through some other stuff."

As I scraped the sauce off my pasta and ate a bite or two, Lisa walked me through some rules regarding the use of the pool, the gym, the beach, and the crafts room. She walked me through the shelter in place protocol for hurricanes, and the evacuation plan in case one ever got bad enough. She even made sure to give me instructions on how and when I could use the table games.

"So that's about it," Lisa finished. "Do you have any questions?"

How long until the hurricane warning is over and I'm free to leave?

"No, I don't think so. Thank you," I said, as a displeased-looking woman from the dining room staff locked one set of doors and turned off all the lights, save for those over the table we were sitting at.

I braced myself for the long event-less night ahead; it was only 8 p.m.

THREAD NINE

―――

The day after the announcement, I was pacing the empty clubhouse's salon back and forth, trying to get my thoughts together. I was stuck in Pembroke. I would probably have stayed in Florida for one or two more weeks finishing Luciano's story, but there was something different about *knowing* I couldn't leave. It made me feel trapped, and I hated being trapped. I hated the feeling of knowing there's nothing I could do to change things.

I dug out the pouch with my money, my grandma's bracelet, and the flash drive from the depths of my purse—it usually just laid there for months undisturbed—and held it in my hands. It was almost as if I could run away from Pembroke with just that pouch and forget I had ever been here. The hell with my job. The hell with everything. I'd fly back home to Costa Rica and go back to the land of Dad paying for everything, beach trips with my friends, of sunshine 365 days a year...

Mom had already called to say I should just go home either way. Never mind me losing my OPT work permit I worked for during all my years in college. She would rather me just be home. But Costa Rica was also, on occasion, the land of appearances, of swallowing things back, of pretending things were okay when, in reality, they weren't. I couldn't give up now, could I?

"Miss Penelope?" A soft, raspy voice interrupted my brainstorming session. It was one of the staff members at Pembroke, and she was holding a folded piece of paper. "This is for you," she said, handing it to me.

"Thank you," I replied, confused. "Who is this from?"

"A, um, a gentleman standing outside by the gates. Visitors can't come in anymore…"

"Right," I said, setting the items in my hands down on the table next to my computer to open the note.

Penelope, it's Peter, Juliana's grandson, the note began. My heart began beating a little faster. *Can you please meet me by the gate? I have something important to tell you.*

That's all he said. No details about what this "something important" was. Or why he wanted to tell *me*. I tapped my foot and bit the inside of my cheek thoughtfully. I couldn't just ignore his request, right? But I shouldn't be excited about it either. And I certainly shouldn't be glad I was wearing my layered pink skirt and a white crop top instead of my exercise clothes from the other day.

I made my way outside and started walking in the heat toward the gate, trying to anticipate why Peter was here. It had to be he had a present for Juliana, something he wanted her to have as a gift. Did she mention when her birthday was? Maybe it was just a gift, for no specific occasion. With these thoughts, I came to the gate and saw Peter's red Jeep Cherokee parked right outside. He was sitting in the driver's seat, looking down at what I assumed was his phone, so he didn't notice me arriving. I stood right in front of his car, on my side of the gate, and crumpled his little note into a ball I threw against the car's windshield to get his attention.

"Penelope!" I heard Peter's deep voice come from inside the car as he jerked back to reality and hopped outside. "Thanks for coming." With the breeze blowing, I caught the faintest scent of beer coming off him.

"At your service," I joked. God damnit.

"I... I guess I have a favor to ask of you," he said, his honey-brown eyes looking down at an envelope he was holding in his left hand.

It was definitely beer. Although we were separated by the gate, we were standing close enough to where I could smell traces of it still lingering in his breath.

"I figured that much," I said, extending my hand through the metallic bars of the gate to accept the envelope from him.

"You'd take this envelope from me, just like that?" Peter asked, taken aback.

"Like what?" I dropped my hand and placed it on my hip.

"You have no clue what's in it or who it's for."

"Given that Juliana is the reason why we know each other and she's your grandma, I assumed..."

"Okay, yeah, it's for her. I guess. Kind of. But you don't want to know what's inside before you carry it off? It could be an explosive. Or worse, a virus that would be released into the air the minute someone opens the package," Peter said, waving the envelope in the air sensationally.

"Hmm," I began, letting my head drop to the side, "I guess I'm not keeping up with YA sci-fi as much as you are. I can't believe I almost released a killer contagion into the air."

"I mean, it does sound a bit paranoid, but you never know..."

"Besides, if I were really *that* curious, I could just open the envelope before giving it to Juliana," I retorted.

"You'd have no clue what to make of what's in it." Peter smiled with satisfaction.

"In that case, would you be as kind as to indulge me by revealing the envelope's top-secret contents?" I asked, giving in.

"It's serious," Peter said, his voice dropping even lower. Actually serious.

I nodded encouragingly, wiping the smile off my face to show him I was serious too.

"I'm doing some research. And I know you were kidding before, but it really is a secret."

"I'm good with secrets," I said, extending my hand across the gate's bars expectantly. "Especially when I'm in on them. Would you mind me asking exactly what sort of research this is?"

Peter, the guy who was usually smiling and joking and talking without giving much thought to what he said, was quiet for a minute. He stared at the envelope in his hand and hugged it to his chest. I dropped my arm down.

"You don't have to tell me," I offered. It was really none of my business. And the less involved I was with Peter, the better.

"But I want to." Peter looked up at me with his beautiful eyes and a softer version of his perfect smile. "Would you mind...?" He gestured toward his car questioningly.

I wanted to get in the car with Peter and hear his secret story. Listen to him hold every sound in his mouth before letting it go gently. I hated being more interested in Peter, whom I'd just met once before, than in Ricky, my boyfriend of over a year.

When we first met, Ricky and I, he was fun to be around. I didn't find him particularly interesting, but he was not as dull as most of the other guys I'd met at Duke. I soon realized both of Ricky's parents were top executives. His dad at a multinational banking company and his mom at a gigantic, packaged food conglomerate. When I first met them, even before Ricky and I were fully dating, they had both been very supportive of my job search and offered to help. I didn't want to take them up on this offer, but after my one-year work permit with the student VISA was over, I figured it wouldn't hurt to know these people in high-up places... Just in case, you know? And Ricky was really not all bad.

"Sure," I replied, going over to the guardhouse and asking Mike—I had finally learned his name—to let me out.

"We can't really—" Mike began.

"I know," I cut him off with a sigh. "What do you want?" I decided I'd get straight to the point.

"No, that's not what I—"

"I know," I stopped him again. "But there must be something I can do for you."

He tilted his head to the side pensively.

"Some food I can get for you," I added, at the risk of leaving the offer too open. "Maybe I can hold the fort down for a while from time to time and you can take a quick break?"

At that, he perked up a little.

"After all, I'll be living here," I continued. "So once in a while, I could just sub in for you and you could go... anywhere really."

"Deal," he said with a nod and an attempt at a wink. I was not a fan of the wink.

I walked out the gate and climbed into the passenger seat of Peter's jeep, surveying the car quickly and realizing it was uncommonly clean for a guy. Save for three empty beer bottles, carefully placed on the floor mat of the passenger seat. It also smelled intensely of some sort of freshener. Forest scented, I think. I shifted the bottles over to the side with my foot as I sat down.

"Shit, I'm sorry about that," Peter said, leaning in closer as he reached for two bottles and moved them to the floor on the back seat.

"It's okay."

"No, no, I got them. I'm sorry." He went on, grabbing the last bottle and also tossing it back.

"So…" I prompted, once Peter was done with the reorganizing.

"This is… um, well, it's hard to tell where to begin." Peter looked down at his hands on the steering wheel.

"Wherever you feel is best," I offered, having no clue what to expect.

"My dad died when I was twenty-three," Peter blurted, looking me straight in the eye.

I definitely did not expect *that*.

"Peter's I'm so s—"

"He… he didn't just die," Peter interrupted before I could finish. "He was murdered."

"Oh my god, that's—"

"I mean, I think he was. The police haven't charged anyone with murder yet. And Grandma thinks it's best to let go of the anger. But I decided I won't stop until I figure out who took Dad away from us. He would've never, ever, just left us."

I looked at him, not knowing what to say. That was horrible. Losing a parent was already bad in itself, but this… I could imagine it being absolutely devastating.

"He disappeared one day. Out of the blue," Peter continued, producing another beer bottle seemingly from thin air and taking a long sip. "I had just finished college and started my first job in the city, New York," he clarified. "Mom and Dad were living down here in Naples. They both worked for this big pharmaceutical company, Lemirk. And one day, Mom called me. She was like 'Peter, I don't want to alarm you, but your dad hasn't been home in a day.'"

"Shit," I said, shaking my head in sympathy.

"I was shocked. Dad would never not come home. Never. Especially not unannounced." Peter shook his head and stopped for a second as his eyes became glassy. "I told Mom I was sure he just had a last-minute work meeting. But he never had to leave town for work. And if he had, he would've called. We started calling all his friends from high school, from college... we even called Aunt Caroline who's out in Switzerland. No one knew anything."

"I... I can't imagine." I tried to be comforting but I knew there was really not much I could say. Except for listening, I could do that.

"I flew down here and helped Mom and Grandma look everywhere. But nothing. Then two months after... his, um... his body showed up near the marshes. He had broken bones and lacerations everywhere. But his company's lawyers started red-taping everything in the investigation, and the medical examiner ruled the cause of death inconclusive. Said he could've been drinking and fallen down, hurting himself. Dad didn't drink though. Not more than the one beer or glass of wine."

"Peter..." I let my words trail.

"So that was it. For them. The detectives and the police and all of them. Even for Mom. After it all happened, she kind of just didn't want to talk about it. About Dad. She didn't want me saying much about his life, let alone anything about his death. And for a while, I just went along with her because it was easier, you know? Just keep on tracking ahead. Grandma would talk more about him, but she thought holding on to 'what ifs' just brought more pain, so I went back to New York,"

Peter said, taking another long sip of his beer. "Do you want some?" he asked, offering the bottle to me.

"No, thanks, I'm good," I said. "And you're driving so..."

"Oh, no, don't worry, those are from a few days ago," he said, gesturing to the back seat. I was almost certain that was a lie.

He continued, "But a few months ago, I couldn't shake the feeling something about the way Dad disappeared was very wrong. I quit my New York job and came here to Naples to ask Mom for help but, of course, she wouldn't hear anything about it. I didn't want to concern Grandma about it either, so I've just been doing research on my own."

"I'm glad you're doing this," I said, giving Peter a soft smile, trying to encourage his perfect one to resurface too. And I meant it. He deserved to find out the truth.

"We all really loved him, you know? I thought Mom did too..." He paused. "Anyway, I left my job at a huge advertising firm up there in New York to work at a tiny one here. But it's not just any tiny advertising agency, the one I'm at right now, it's one right next door to the local police department..."

"So you're sneaking in and getting information from their computers?" I asked. The mystery-novel lover in me perking up.

"No! There are cameras everywhere now, silly!" Peter replied, finally cracking a smile.

"But... where are these files you just gave me from?"

"The police department." He grinned mischievously.

"You're making me think you took down one of the detectives there and stole his ID to get in."

"Ha! That's actually not a bad idea... But I'll confess my strategy: I befriended the front-desk clerk. She works the night shift when there are not many people around, and she's able to sneak into one computer or the other once in a while and get me some information."

"Clever," I admitted. "How much did you have to flirt with her to get those?"

Peter looked at me teasingly. "It comes naturally, see?" He demonstrated with a wink.

"Real funny." I smiled.

"But really, in all seriousness," Peter began, placing his hand lightly on my knee, "thank you so much. You'll be helping me out a ton here."

"Wait, what time is it?" I asked, jerking away from his touch as I suddenly remembered I agreed to a call Ricky this afternoon. I had already rescheduled our call a million times and he said it was important. I couldn't push it off again. Could I? I couldn't.

"4:17 p.m. Is... what's up?" Peter asked, bringing his hand back to the steering wheel to rest next to the other.

"Shit. I... I have a call. At four. I have to get going," I said, fumbling around to collect my phone and the envelope before practically jumping out of the car.

"Wait. Can you give me your number?" My heart fluttered. "To explain about the files? I need you to ask Grandma something but she can't exactly know..."

"Sure." I stuck my belongings under my left armpit and took the phone he was offering me, typed up my number quickly, and ran to Mike's guardhouse to get him to let me back in.

I took a deep breath as I dialed Ricky, while I wondered—hoped—if I typed my number correctly into Peter's phone.

PART 2

THREAD TEN

——

I got a *"this is peter"* text right after giving him my number.

I started speaking with Ricky. He suggested I move into his apartment at Duke while the hurricane passed. He thought I should fly out as soon as possible before things got worse. There was talk about airports shutting down, town borders closing up… Mom had also called yesterday night to suggest, yet again, I return home, to Costa Rica. In between these calls and thinking, I forgot to text Peter back, so I got another message from an unsaved number—I have yet to save his number—this morning:

I know it's a weird ask, but can you see if Grandma remembers my dad's phone number? I erased everything… Anyway, it's at the top of those files I gave you. I just need to verify it's his. Then, in a separate text: *And don't show her the files, it's best she doesn't know.*

I sat on my apartment's balcony, drinking my coffee as I read the text. I upgraded from a view of an extended-stay hotel's parking lot to that of a blue ocean, with sunlight dancing off its surface. Not bad. It was definitely a weird ask if Juliana was not supposed to know Peter was sort of investigating this. Especially coming from me. I had no clue how to bring it up to her casually.

Sure, I texted back, swirling my coffee mug thoughtfully and releasing its aroma into the morning's salt-tinted breeze. Another great upgrade from the smoke-scented room. I also kept going back to the conversations with Ricky and Mom. There was no real point in even considering leaving because Adrienne said I couldn't and that was that. But I also had to admit the tiniest part of me almost wanted to stay. To ensure I kept my job and did it as well as possible, yes, but there was something else. Something about Peter and his investigation. Something I couldn't fully explain yet.

I was feeling my coffee's bitter yet pleasant sting when I bolted upright, remembering I left my pouch on the table yesterday afternoon. I had placed both my computer and my pouch on a table in the clubhouse salon to go speak with Peter. And after having walked away from him to speak with Ricky, I picked up my computer on the way back to my room. But somehow, probably because I was distracted by Ricky's great idea of having me fly up to Duke and shutting myself in a house with him and his frat bros for what? Weeks? Months? Anyway, I forgot to pick up my pouch and went straight to my room. I now chugged what remained of my coffee, pulled a light cardigan over my pajamas, and plucked my bag from the sofa. I hurried out of my room and prayed I would find my pouch there. No one really stole things around here and, although not ideal, I guess I'd be fine with them taking the money. But not the bracelet and the flash drive. Please not the flash drive.

I rushed down the stairs so I wouldn't have to wait for the elevator and power-walked through the gardens and into the clubhouse. I zoomed through the main salon in a straight line directly toward the table. My pouch was laying on it, undisturbed. I picked it up, unzipped it, verified all of its contents were still intact, and hugged it to my chest. I stood there for a second, getting myself together, and as I turned to leave, I realized what seemed like a background noise was actually someone speaking to me.

"Penelope," Juliana said. "Is everything okay? After the whole hurricane announcement and everything?"

"Yes, it is," I replied, instinctively bringing my pouch down, clasping it behind my back, and giving her the best damn smile I could muster. Juliana had been sitting on the salon's sofa, holding a tiny needle in one of her hands and sewing what seemed to be a flower onto a patch of cloth.

I hadn't seen Juliana since last Sunday when she introduced me to her grandson, but so much had happened since then. I had nearly forgotten what she'd said to me on the beach. But now I also knew she had lost almost everyone who mattered to her. And now, as a favor to Peter, I was the one in charge of getting information from her to help his investigation. Despite the cold-hearted, careless bitch she made me out to be, I had actually meant to apologize about our conversation that day on the beach.

"Who had ever thought we might have to evacuate Pembroke again? You know we had to about six months ago?" Juliana asked, apparently in the mood for talking.

The fact she didn't call attention to me being in my pajamas and looking like a hurricane myself was oddly comforting. I walked toward her and took a seat on an armchair next to the sofa she was sitting on.

"I've actually been meaning to..." I began, clearing my throat. "I'm sorry if I was rude to you before when we had that conversation on the beach. I didn't mean to be... disrespectful."

"That's all right, sweetie, don't go around worrying yourself," Juliana said, the sparkles dancing in her eyes again as she reached out to place one of her hands over mine. "I'm just glad you actually listened to me. You really do remind me of... of my daughter. I never told her those things and, well, I don't think I will anymore."

The fact she didn't apologize for having been way too severe with someone she didn't know pissed me off, but I settled for giving her a smiling nod and nestling my pouch back into its safe place at the bottom of my handbag.

"I'm sorry you don't speak to her anymore," I said, just as my mind began coming up with an idea on how to switch the topic *and* satisfy my curiosity. Ever since I had seen Juliana walking with Luciano on the beach that morning, I had wondered about them. So I swallowed my lingering annoyance. "I wanted to ask you about Luciano; how to get him to open up more and everything. You seem to be pretty close. Are you and him friends or..."

"Friends." Juliana gave me a tight-lipped smile. "I'll let you get back to your work," she noted, before walking off. Through the glass doors, I saw her disappearing into the shade of a tree.

"Wait!" I called out after her, although I knew she couldn't hear me anymore. I wanted to ask her about Peter's dad's number. When I went out into the gardens, she was nowhere in sight. It was if she'd been magically whisked away by the afternoon breeze somewhere far, far away.

* * *

Later that day when I was eating at The Palms' dining room alone, too absorbed in my notes to notice who was around, I heard a plate scratching the surface of the table in front of me. It was Juliana's. She had taken a seat across from me on the long table and had just moved her plate of food, untouched, out of the way. Probably to get my attention.

"Luciano's wife, his latest ex-wife, is called... um, Emily. No, wait, Amelia. That's her name."

I stared at her intently, somewhat startled by her sudden and seemingly uncalled for offering of information.

"Earlier today you asked about us and I..." she began, combing her silver hair with her delicate fingers. "I sort of avoided the question. No one has ever asked me about him. I've never told anyone. Anyway, it doesn't matter. I guess I was just embarrassed and caught off guard."

"I'm sorry I asked. You don't have to tell me," I said, suddenly ashamed I'd been so blunt in prying into her life. What was I thinking? I had to stick to asking what I had to, not things that were none of my business.

"It's okay. I want to," Juliana declared, pulling her plate closer and poking two potatoes with her fork before laying it back down on the plate to continue. "When Luciano first got here, he was still married to that woman. Amelia, that's it. Only I didn't know that. Rob had died." She paused, looking down at her stacked potatoes. "I think it was almost five, actually more like ten years ago, and I thought maybe I was ready," she said, finally biting into the potatoes.

I just stared back, somewhat bewildered but also entertained.

"We were becoming friends, Luciano and I, but he soon started coming to me for advice on how to deal with Amelia. His wife. He was furious at her because she had him committed to Pembroke after his surgery of, how do you call it?

"The heart?" I offered.

"No, no, on his leg...?"

"Knee?"

"Yes, knee surgery. His wife said the recovery would be 'too much' for her to deal with. She's some twenty or thirty years younger than him and, from what I gather, she wanted the freedom to travel and party without... Well, without an old man." She chuckled.

"That hurts."

"Oh, and that was only the beginning. He later learned she was having an affair."

"That's not okay," I commented, looking down at my own half-eaten plate.

"But only after she discovered *he* had been having an affair too."

"Shit." I shook my head. "Sorry," I corrected myself quickly, "I mean, that's too bad."

Juliana laughed. "You can swear in front of me, Penelope, I couldn't really care less." I noticed for the first time, when Juliana smiled, a small dimple, an almost imperceptible dent, appeared on her left cheek. "It was all downhill after that. He filed for divorce right then and there, and I was his friend throughout the whole process. Needless to say, by the end of it, I knew too much and had lost interest in him. As anything other than a friend."

"I know a few guys like that. My friend Liam in college," I found myself sharing out loud. "I had the biggest crush on him when I first met him and then... let's just say he told me something about a girl he was with and I realized I never wanted to be that girl."

It was weird, how Juliana inspired this desire in me to share. I would normally wait for others to ask before I shared, especially when I was on writing assignments. And I had never brought up hooking up casually to an old woman. Things just came out with Juliana. She had a way of making you feel like she saw you. Not just the crumb laying on your top lip or the stray hair hanging down your face. She saw the real you, and she wanted to understand you.

"That's men for you! Luciano is an amazing artist and a very interesting person, though. I'm really happy you're speaking to him. If there's one thing he's great at, it's speaking about himself!"

I suddenly found myself kind of liking Juliana.

"Oh, before I forget, Peter's putting together some sort of memorial... I don't really know. He's just wondering if you remember, um, your son's phone number." I opened the handbag on my knees beneath the table and pulled out a notepad and pen. I kept the file Peter had given me hidden in my bag and peeked into it for the first time. I opened it carefully underneath the table to keep Juliana from seeing it and asking more questions. *It was already such an uncomfortable thing to ask: can I please have your dead son's phone number?*

"You've been talking?" Juliana asked. "You and Peter, I mean?"

I began nodding and felt my eyes widening as I saw a small line at the top of the file, stating the phone number. Everything beneath it was marked out by giant, repeating, bolded words: *Confidential.*

"You are?" Juliana prompted.

"Yes," I said, coming back to it and looking at her. "He asked for my help to..." I didn't really know what else to say.

"555-422-2560," Juliana recited, almost as if she had repeated his number to herself a million times each night. She probably had.

I glanced down at the file on my lap while I pretended to scribble the number she gave me on my notepad. It matched the number on the records.

"Thanks," I said. "I know it's a weird ask but—"

"Penelope," Juliana began, placing one of her cold little hands on top of mine. "I'm glad you're helping Peter." And she gave me a beautifully dimpled smile.

THREAD ELEVEN

The afternoon sun was spilling golden rays all over Pembroke's gardens, drowning them in an air of lazy delight. I sat down on one of the tables and decided it was actually time to make progress on my Luciano story. We had two sessions so far, and I definitely had enough to get started. Plus, I wanted to get some writing done before... I don't actually know before what.

My mom was getting anxious about me not going back to Costa Rica as things with the hurricane got progressively worse. And I was running out of ways to tell Ricky there was no way I'd be leaving Pembroke but, if I did, I would never go live with him and his bros. So I just wanted to write and prove to myself I was doing the right thing by staying. *The right thing for who, though?* I often wondered what I was really fighting for. A chance to work in the US? It was more than that.

With these thoughts running through my mind, I was not as focused as I wanted to be, and I saw myself breaking my number one rule when writing: don't look at my phone.

A Snapchat from Lara, my New York roommate, saying she wished I was back in our apartment so she didn't have to be there all alone watching TV instead of going out.

A text from Alice saying the subject of her feature story, the baseball player, was having a meltdown over the possibility of his upcoming season being postponed because of an ankle fracture. An absolute curl-up-in-couch-watching-old-games-and-eating-ice-cream sort of meltdown.

I had to laugh at that one. Life at Pembroke had been weirdly undisturbed by the approaching hurricane, except for the lack of visitors. I had overheard some nurses complaining, *"As if being stuck with old-ass people for ten hours a day is not already painful enough... now we don't get to flirt with their sons! And did you hear about the possible layoffs?"*

Word had also reached me about Luxury L.S. furloughing some employees for an indefinite time. The magazine was going through some financial difficulties, Adrienne told us via an online conference call, and they were really relying on our pieces to bring readership back up. I had to make sure it was not me getting fired, because if my days of unemployment started accumulating, I would risk losing my stupid work permit, and...

Which reminded me, I had to write. But my phone buzzed with a text from an unsaved number.

Hi, the text said, and I couldn't help but be excited when I opened it and saw the conversation history, verifying it was Peter.

I could see the little bubbles showing he was typing something, but after a few seconds, the bubbles stopped. I drummed my finger slightly on the side of my laptop as I waited for him to send the message, but when nothing came up, I decided to respond with a simple: *Hi.*

I've got more info on the investigation. Can I stop by? he finally texted.

Sure, I typed up quickly. *When?*
Now?

Now as in you're about to drive over, or now as in you're already on the way?

Now as in I'm out here by the gate.

Oh, great. Just what I needed when I was about to get back to being productive, I lied to myself. I wondered what he intended to share with me this time. I stuffed my laptop into my bag and made my way out to the entrance. It was starting to get cool enough for me to have to pull out my cardigan and wrap myself in it. As I got closer to the entrance, I saw Peter's red Jeep parked outside and him pacing next to it with another envelope in his hands. When he looked up and saw me approaching, Peter flashed one of his perfect smiles.

"I'll really owe you big time, Penelope," he called out, coming up to the gate. "I may have to buy you lunch. Hell, even dinner I think."

"I'd be content with just chocolates," I said, leaning against my side of the gate once I got there.

"Really? Done."

"No, no, I'm kidding," I assured him. "I like helping out with this, I promise."

"Did I interrupt you just now? From whatever it is you do here?" Peter asked.

"Not really," I lied. "And for your information, what I do here are interviews and writing."

"That's amazing. Why don't you tell me more about—?"

"Why, um, why did his phone records have a 'classified' stamp?" I blurted. I was planning on making a plan about how to bring up the question very casually in conversation, but Peter texting me he was out here already gave me little time to prepare the plan. This had to do.

"You looked through the files?" Peter asked, raising both his eyebrows.

"Well, I opened them to see the number at the top. I'm sorry if—"

"No, don't be. I just don't want to pull you into this whole mess... I mean, I know I'm doing just that, but I just need you to help me verify some stuff with Grandma without her realizing what I'm doing."

"Are you kidding? I enjoy mysteries and I've always wanted to help solve one." I knew getting involved was not the best thing to do, but I would really love to help figure a mystery out, to shed light on the truth.

Peter stared into space blankly without giving me a response, but I could be stubborn when I wanted something, and now I wanted to help.

"So," I said, trying to edge him back on track, "why the classified stamp?"

"I'm not sure," Peter replied, untucking the new envelope from under his arm and looking down at it. "There's even more."

"Can I see?" I asked, extending my arm through the gate's metal bars.

After what seemed like a long pause, Peter knelt on the ground on his side of the gate. He opened the file he was holding and spread a few pieces of paper on the paved driveway. I knelt on my side and read what I could.

I picked up the first document titled *Email records*. There was a stamp under it saying *Classified*, just like the phone records in Peter's first file. I picked up the second document titled *Computer records*. Also followed by a *Classified* stamp.

"What the fuck?" I said into the air.

"I know," Peter agreed, shaking his head. "Read this one," he added, handing me another file titled *Interview with Danny*

Morales, co-worker. For a second, I thought he wouldn't let go of the document but he did.

Police: So tell me about your relationship with Santiago.

So that is—was—his name. Up to this point, I had only thought of him as "Peter's dad" or "Juliana's son." Knowing his name made it all much more real.

Subject: We were good friends. We loved going out for hikes. And brunch. We went to brunch with our wives every other week.

Police: Where do you know Santiago from?

Subject: Work. We both worked at Lemirk's—

Lawyer: He can't reveal any additional information there.

Police: Can he tell us what they were working on?

Lawyer: Yes. The R&D department.

Police: Danny, can you be more specific?

Lawyer: He can't. That's the only publicly available information, so that's all you can get.

Police: Okay. Let's try this. Can you tell us about his character? What was he like as a person?

Subject: Probably the most interesting person I've known. He was always coming up with new ideas to try. Always smiling. And always ready for an adventure.

"Let me spare you the rest," Peter said, grabbing the document back from my hands. "It basically says nothing else. That stupid company lawyer didn't let him say anything."

"I'm so confused. Why can't the police know what he was working on?"

"Apparently they can't even know what Danny thinks of him leaving early the day he disappeared. The lawyer didn't allow him to respond saying it's 'speculative.'"

"This is so frustrating. I'm sorry," I said, gathering up the papers that were on the ground on my side of the gate and handing them back to Peter. "Did you try speaking to Danny yourself? Like calling him or something?"

"Of course. But all I got is he got a divorce and married a woman from Georgia and moved out there with her. The other co-worker who gave me that information also gave me his supposed new number. But it was disconnected when I tried it."

"Damn it."

"Look at this note," Peter said, shifting through the papers and handing one back to me. I could see his mind was in a million different places now. "This was at the top of Dad's case file. And it basically says no questions can be asked. Not by the police. Not by me."

The note read: *These records are protected as part of Lemirk's proprietary information. Under no circumstances should they be accessed by anyone outside of the company. Failure to comply may result in charges adding up to a ten million dollar fine and up to thirty years in prison.*

"It's like a giant 'fuck you' to the police," I said, shaking my head. "And you, of course."

"I just wish there was something I could hold onto, you know?" Peter said, looking down at the worthless pieces of paper, saying it more to himself than to me.

"I know," I replied, although I truly didn't. Without even knowing what I was doing, I reached out and gave his arm a little squeeze.

Peter's eyes opened a little wider as they followed my hand, but before he could look back up and meet my eyes, I jerked my hand back and grabbed the envelope he brought.

"What should I do with these?" I asked. "You want me to ask Juliana something, right?"

"Yes. Please. Don't show them to her, though. Can you just ask her about the policeman in that interview I just showed you? She talked to him after, I remember, and I think he told her something about the conversation with Danny and the lawyers."

I nodded as a question began forming in my head: why did Peter want my help here? Why not go to Juliana himself? Visitors were not allowed, but he could just call her. He had mentioned not wanting to bother or concern her, but I didn't see how bringing me in—someone who didn't know anything about what had happened—helped. *Perhaps that is exactly it.*

"Thanks, Penelope," Peter said. I could feel his eyes smiling at me even if his mouth didn't. He got up from the ground and began patting his pants to get the dust off them.

I was putting the envelope into my bag and getting ready to get up from the ground too when my hand brushed against my special pouch, laying at the bottom of the bag.

"Wait," I said, as yet another idea began taking shape. "What if your dad left more information behind?"

"What do you mean?" Peter asked, kneeling back down.

"Well, um, let's see: if there was information that *really* mattered to me, I'd carry it around everywhere. In, say, something like a flash drive in a pouch, you know?"

"Hm, I see… oddly specific." He flashed a smile before becoming serious again. "So you're saying maybe he kept a copy of some of his records?"

"He could have. Did he carry something around with him all the time?"

"Nothing specific. Not that I can remember," Peter huffed, letting out a heavy sigh. "But why would he keep an extra copy either way?"

"I don't know, I'm just saying…" I shrugged. "Anyway, I have to get going to do that writing I was telling you about. Let me know if you have anything else. And I'll let you know what I can get from Juliana."

"How long has it been? I hope I didn't keep you too long from your writing."

"It's okay," I said, standing up and dusting off the back of my shorts.

Peter came up too and hesitated briefly, before walking over to his car and getting in. He started backing out of Pembroke's entrance and I began walking back, but I heard the car's motor stop.

"Hey, Penelope!" he said, sticking his head out the Jeep's window. "I'll see if something comes to mind. About where he could've kept some information."

With that and before waiting for my response, he drove off, leaving behind a cloud of dust that levitated in the air for a minute before being swallowed again by the afternoon's heat.

THREAD TWELVE

———

"Why don't you play a little with the light?" Luciano suggested, standing behind me. We were in the art studio the morning after my conversation with Peter.

Luciano had finally convinced me to paint his subject of choice: a forest with a woman in it. Except there was no woman in it yet, and no forest. Just a few scattered trees. I decided to draw a tree's shadow to "play with the lighting" and satisfy Luciano's desires so he wouldn't nag at me so much.

I was doing some soft, circular strokes with gray paint on the ground below my tree when my thoughts drifted to yesterday's conversation with Peter. He said he wanted me to stay on the periphery of the investigation, but something in the way his eyes lit up when I started asking him questions told me otherwise.

"That looks like a hole!" Luciano exclaimed, interrupting my thoughts and snatching the paintbrush from my hand, as if trying to prevent me from sinking deeper into a hole of chaos.

I had forgotten he was standing behind me while he waited for a layer in his forest's sky to dry. I liked it much more when he was painting too and less vigilant of my brush's every stroke.

"Can I have that back?" I asked, eager to do something to fix my shadow which did, in fact, look like a hole.

"Try using more diffused shadows. They're the ones that don't come from a direct light source. It makes the shadows more real," Luciano explained, all while holding my brush in his hand as if it were a baton.

When he finished, he handed it back to me and sat down in front of his own canvas. "See," he said, making tiny, dark green strokes to the side of his tree.

"I see."

"Also, don't use black."

"What do you mean? Shadows are black," I countered.

"Not exactly. Shadows exist in nature. They're a combination of many colors, and they may look something like black. But they're never *truly* black."

"I could've sworn—" I began, about to contradict him.

"Plus, the whole point of shadows is to accentuate light," he interjected. "They shouldn't be there to hide elements in your painting, but rather to point us to the ones we should be looking at."

"That actually makes a lot of sense," I mused, beginning to mix dark greens, blues, and browns in my color palette.

"Good. I'm glad it does. Now let me tell you about the first painting I ever finished," Luciano began.

This was my cue to pull out the notepad and begin taking notes, so I did.

"It was a meadow. I called it *Pomeriggio Soleggiato in un Prato*, or *Sunny Afternoon in a Meadow*. I finished grade school in my hometown of Verino and was accepted at the *Accademia di Belle Arti di Firenze*. My professors were so impressed by my mastery over the *impasto* and *chiaroscuro* techniques, but they said my painting was missing *something*."

Luciano emphasized this last word, making a dramatic pink stroke on his painting's sky.

"I wonder what—"

"I was frustrated with them for not telling me what that *something* was. They said they still didn't know. So I spent the next few weeks partying with my friends and skipping class. And it was at a café one afternoon after a long night out drinking I met Marietta. We were introduced by mutual friends. She was wearing a crisp, white and blue striped dress and a handkerchief tied around her black curls," Luciano said, with a tenderness in his voice I hadn't heard before. He paused here, took a long sip of coffee from his mug, and returned his attention to his painting and the story.

"I learned she was a poet, and she was sharing her newest piece with her friends. I couldn't hear the whole piece as she read it out loud in her small, melodic voice, but I was mesmerized by what I did hear. She was able to stretch an image, of a girl picking flowers, in all shapes and directions until it revealed the girl's inner conflict about marrying the older man her parents wanted her to. I felt an instant connection as soon as I heard her laugh for the first time; a genuine, guttural laugh."

I let out a "hm" and raised my eyebrows, suddenly feeling a bit skeptical. I realized this was the first time I'd spoken to Luciano after hearing Juliana tell me he had cheated on his third wife and ended yet another marriage. *How long after meeting this Marietta that he claims to have loved so dearly did he cheat on her?*

"That night, I didn't go out," Luciano continued. "I woke up early the next morning and walked around campus in search of Marietta. And there she was, sitting at the steps of the library with a book in her lap, waiting for the building to open."

Luciano looked up at me expectantly, and I managed to give him a smile. That seemed like encouragement enough for him to go on, so he did.

"With Marietta, I learned what love was and how it felt to really feel it. What I had felt for Marina was infatuation from afar. With Marietta, it was up close and tangible: it was true love. I finally understood what the *something* missing in my paintings was. It was love."

Tender, I thought, glancing down at my phone. I saw a text from Peter he sent about an hour ago: *Anything yet?*

No, I typed back. *You?*

No.

"I soon realized the girl picking flowers in Marietta's poems was her." Luciano went on, adding tiny, delicate pink petals on a flower growing in his forest. "We eloped and got married before her parents could force her to marry that older man. And we were as happy as anyone could be. We spent summers at the coast, reading and writing by the ocean and making love when the sun set."

"What a life."

"It was indeed!" Luciano responded with a smile, which made me think he didn't pick up on the note of sarcasm in my comment. I had to give it to him though, he was a romantic at heart.

"We had our first child, a beautiful girl named Gloria with the most gorgeous hazel eyes. My paintings were thriving in the local market, and they were even starting to get international attention. I got invited to an artistic conference in Paris in 1969. Marietta stayed behind to teach the poetry class she had begun teaching, but when I came back from Paris two months or so after, I realized something had changed. The energetic fervor that drove Marietta's discussions about art and her passion for life had begun dwindling. She was quieter, and things seemed old and boring to her, instead of always new and interesting," Luciano explained with a deep sigh. He shook his head and stared at his canvas wistfully.

"I took her to the doctor and we learned she was pregnant again. The doctor comforted me, saying sometimes women's hormones change drastically during pregnancy but normalize after it. I held on to this assessment desperately until the day she went into labor. That day, my heart broke." Luciano brought his hand, still holding a paintbrush, to his chest and looked down at the floor.

"Marietta didn't make it. And the thing she expelled from her body, that thing that had eaten her up from the insides, was stillborn."

THREAD THIRTEEN

———

I thanked Luciano for the art session and headed downstairs. He said he'd stay behind to finish some stuff up. As I walked into the clubhouse's salon, I found Juliana sitting on the sofa I had last seen her on. She was sewing again. The one-petaled flower had multiplied into three bright yellow ones.

"Hi, Penelope," Juliana said. I wondered how she knew it was me if she hadn't looked up from her sewing. "How are you?"

"Good, good." I sat down on the armchair across her. Then, to make enough conversation to eventually ask what I had to, I added, "The hurricane's supposed to be picking up strength, did you hear?"

"The hurricane...?" She stared at me blankly for a moment.

"Yes. The hurricane that's approaching—"

"Oh, yes, yes, of course. Have you ever been through one?" she asked, looking up from the sunflowers. Maybe they were other types of yellow flowers, I couldn't tell.

"No, I haven't. My mom wants me to go home but..."

"Where's home?" Juliana asked, shifting her small frame on the sofa to face me directly.

"Costa Rica."

"Wow, I didn't know that! That's amazing. Rob and I went to visit there for one of the kids' breaks from school. They were around eight and ten, I think. We loved it. Some of the best memories with my kids honestly."

"That's good to hear. Most people I talk to have had great experiences in Costa Rica and they can't believe I left 'paradise,'" I scoffed.

"People said the same to me about Brazil." Juliana smiled. "I get it though. It's not all as wonderful as it seems."

Here was Juliana again, making me feel understood. I kind of wanted to hug her and feel the comforting fabric of her knitted sweater on my arms.

"Exactly," I said, interlacing my fingers, not knowing what to do with them while Juliana's worked so diligently on a green leaf. "I want to hear the story," I added resolutely, almost surprising myself.

"Which one?" Juliana's head shifted slightly to the side and her green eyes lit up with excitement. This reaction made asking her worth it.

"The one about Rob. About how you met." *The one I had not paid attention to that other day because I was too busy thinking about my fucking self.*

"Oh, *that* story. Of course." She put her needle down, interlaced her fingers on top of her lap, and looked at me. "So I told you about how I was stubborn and decided I had to go to the US for college despite my parents wanting me to stay at home? And how I ended up at Berkeley?"

"Yes."

"Well, I loved Berkeley and I thrived in that atmosphere. I went to all those protests and I wore one of those flower crowns on my head," Juliana said, padding her now short, silver hair down softly. "My mom was horrified when she first came to visit. She hated those rags I wore as clothes," she said, smiling at the memory.

"So you became a full sixties' hippy?"

"Could a well-to-do foreigner who was raised to be a lady her whole life really help it?" Juliana joked back.

"Good point." I grinned.

"Mom would not have it that way, so she decided to spend a few months up there in the San Francisco area with me. Like any proper wife of a politician would, she rented an apartment by the San Francisco Bay with incredible views. And, of course, she began looking for a chauffeur to drive her around. She asked the University to post an announcement on the main letter board and she soon had a taker. Care to guess who?"

"Rob?"

"Yes, Rob! I didn't know him, but apparently, he had first noticed me during a class we both took: Ancient Greek Political Thought. He was not a Classics major, but he had chosen this class as an elective. I always sat in the front, so I didn't notice the tall, brown-eyed guy in the back of the class with neatly combed hair and button-down shirts. At the time, I was not really interested in neatly combed guys with button-down shirts, to be honest."

I nodded at her encouragingly. She was a great storyteller. The tone of her voice, her pauses... I wanted to hear more.

"Rob said when he saw the announcement, he recognized my name and called the number immediately to take the job. I later learned he did not need the money. Anyway, Rob started driving my mom and me around and when he dropped her off at her apartment and took me back to campus, on those car rides back alone, we started falling in love."

"I love this. Your story, I mean."

"It's about to get crazy, just wait!" Juliana exclaimed eagerly.

"Let's hear it," I replied, legitimately excited.

"So we had this fun, flirtatious dynamic but hadn't started dating seriously. And quite suddenly, my grandfather became very ill back in Brazil. He barely survived a heart attack, but the doctors said he probably didn't have much time left. So I was, naturally, flown back home in the middle of my fall semester."

"Were you able to freeze your classes and finish later?" I asked, the academic in me ever so concerned.

Juliana laughed. "I guess I never even thought of that! My parents said it was time for me to go back home for a while. More for like an indefinite period though. And I never went back to college after that."

"I'm sorry."

"I am too. But those were other times. My parents didn't see much... value, I think, in me getting a college education. Least of all one which transformed me into a hippie."

"Truly other times..."

"Anyway, my dad, I told you he was a diplomat. So he had to tend to some business or other in New York. My mom wanted to stay back in Brazil with her dad, so I was designated as dad's companion and off I went back to the US, but this time to the East Coast.

"Little did I know at the time Rob had heard news of me leaving Berkley and he was upset. 'Devastated and utterly destroyed,' he described his state of mind when he told me the story himself much later. He took the first flight to Brazil he could find, without even knowing where I lived. The world was smaller back then though, and after a few interrogations here and there, he came upon my house, only to learn that I'd left for New York."

"Stop, that's crazy! He just chased you out to Brazil without having a clue if he'd ever find you!"

"That he did. And then, well, he flew to New York to meet me there. But alas when he got to the hotel my dad and I had been staying at, I had flown back to Brazil." Juliana moved her hands theatrically as she recounted the story with sparkles in her eyes.

"Don't tell me that…"

"He did; he went back to Brazil! Oh, I was so happy when I saw him. I had thought of him a bit, I'll admit, but I assumed when I left Berkley, that was it for us. But here he was, in my home, telling me he had traveled the world for me and would do it again a thousand times if that's what was necessary for me to see how much he loved me."

"This is so romantic, Juliana. I don't even think I ever believed this type of fairy-tale love was real," I said, looking into her eyes.

"We got married soon after and I moved to New York with him. He had begun working at the… that international agency? The UN. Their Security Council. Rob's parents had come from Cuba before things got bad there, and he committed himself to a diplomatic career to make some sense of the world. He was an idealist back then, and he never stopped being one. And after New York, we traveled the world on diplomatic missions. Paris. Japan. Everywhere."

"I've always wanted to travel like that. I've been to Paris and the big cities, but it's different now. And I've only been to them as a tourist. What you did sounds so much more… fancy and exclusive."

"It was. We were in cocktail parties with all the big names at the time. But I was getting old. Can you imagine? Old at twenty-one? Anyway, my parents started reminding me not so subtly it was time to have babies. So Rob and I settled back in New York and we had Santiago. And just two years after we had my baby girl. And… well, yes, that's the story of how I met Rob."

"That's… thanks for telling me," I sighed. That was such an amazing love story. Wow. "But, how did you know? It sounds so cheesy, but how did you know Rob was *the one*?"

Juliana looked down at her wrinkled hands, which were once again resting on her lap, and then up at the ceiling. A smile started creeping up into her thin, pink lips and extending into her cheeks, exposing their dimples. Finally, she leveled her gaze with mine and looked straight into my eyes.

"You know how I knew Rob was the one I wanted to marry?" she asked, rhetorically.

"How?"

"Because we told each other story after story, night after night. We always had a new story to share with the other." Juliana smiled into the salon's stuffy afternoon air, reminiscing.

"I thought you were going to say something about true love. Or unconditional love," I said, turning to face her and hoping she'd catch my allusion to our very first conversation about Greek Mythology.

"But it does have everything to do with love, Penelope," Juliana replied with a note of indignation.

"So you're saying being able to tell stories is a sign of love?"

"Being able to tell stories *is* love. All great loves are about stories. First, the ones you tell each other, and then the ones you build together."

I bit my bottom lip musingly and squinted my eyes at her, trying to fully absorb and conceptualize what she was saying.

"The way I see it, we are each a thread. We are born, small and simple, as a single thread. And we start relating with our parents and our threads start crossing over and weaving the family portion of our blanket. Then we make a best friend. We start talking and sharing about our lives and start crossing our life thread with that of this friend into the friendship portion of our blanket. Same goes for every relationship we form. We start intertwining the thread of our life with the thread of theirs. With Rob, it was easy to walk through the different sections of my blanket and bring him into them. It was even easier to start creating a new section of our own."

"I see..." I replied, thinking it through. I loved her choice of metaphor. Poetic.

"Can I tell you something?" Juliana asked, suddenly shy.

"Yes. Of course."

"I knew I wanted to share the thread of my story with you from the first moment we exchanged a word with each other."

"And why was that?" I asked, truly surprised. I had, after all, been pretty mean.

"Well, because your name is Penelope, of course!" Juliana moved her hand over to my shoulder to give it a light squeeze. "I'm kidding. Maybe not completely. But it was not only your name. It's the questions you ask."

"What about them?"

"They keep the yarn spinning."

We talked a little more before I stood up from the armchair to head out, but I remembered what I had promised Peter I'd ask her and stood there for a moment before walking away.

"This might seem random," I started, "but do you remember a policeman who you talked to about, um, Santiago? The one who told you about Danny and the lawyers and that odd conversation?"

"Danny...?" Juliana tilted her head and smiled.

"Yes, Santiago's work friend," I said, sitting back down.

"Oh, yes, yes. I remember Danny."

"But do you remember the policeman who told you about his interrogation with the lawyers?"

"Interrogation?" Juliana asked again. She had absolutely no clue what I was talking about.

"Yes. Right before they interrogated you."

"Hmm," Juliana said in response and went back to her stitching. I decided to leave it at that.

* * *

"It was in the microscope case."

These were the first words that came out of my phone's speaker when I, semi-consciously, picked it up at 3:04 a.m. I'd been up until around two in the morning working on the Luciano article, and I'd probably just fallen asleep when I heard the phone.

"Peter?" I asked, recognizing his voice's deep notes.

"Yes, sorry, hello, you were right!" he said, his words all strung together with an inhuman amount of energy for this time of night.

"About what?" I said, finally sitting up straight and turning on the night lamp.

"You said, maybe, there was something he carried around all the time."

"Oh—"

"And I realized it was his microscope! It was the first one he ever owned. The one his dad got for him when he was a boy."

"He carried a microscope around everywhere?" The guy was a scientist, yes, but carrying a microscope everywhere seemed like a little much.

"He called it Mr. Scope. And it's not very big, but he did bring it around everywhere. I remember I used to think it was sort of weird he always took it with us when we went on family trips to like the mountains or something. He said he wanted to have it close just in case he found something cool."

"I guess—"

"We used it, once in a while, to examine the wings of a butterfly we found on our porch or the skeleton of a leaf. But yesterday after we talked, I started going through his stuff that's with me because Mom didn't want it. And I saw a picture of us on the 'Take your Children to Work Day' at Lemirk when I was around fifteen. I remember being annoyed I had to go… Anyway, he was loading Mr. Scope into the car's trunk, and I remember asking him why he needed Mr. Scope at work if there were so many better quality microscopes there."

"Yeah, that is odd."

"He said it was like his muse. He liked to bring Mr. Scope to work to remind himself to be inspired and never stop being curious… I don't even know. It was some dumb excuse that, to my fifteen-year-old self, just sounded like my dad was a science nerd. But yesterday I thought maybe…"

"Was there something?"

"A compact hard drive. "

"Oh, my God," I breathed, bringing my hand up to my mouth in disbelief.

"It has everything, Penelope. I haven't been able to look too much because I just found it and had to call you, but it looks like he backed everything up into it."

"Wow, this is… amazing."

"I know. It could all be in here."

"I really hope we find something."

"We will."

"I just don't want you to get your hopes up and then—"

"We just have to figure out what to look for. I'm sure it will be here."

"Okay. I believe in you," I replied, trying to hide my skepticism. When he said it was "all" in there, that probably meant hundreds of millions of files. And we had to find something that resembled a clue amongst it all.

"I believe in *us*," Peter said, emphasizing the "us," and I could almost see a smile stretching across his lips as he said it.

"Oh and one last thing," I said, twirling my hair around my finger. "Juliana didn't remember that cop in the interrogation room with Danny and the lawyer."

"That's odd, I remember her telling me they bonded over loving hot chocolate more than coffee..."

"I'm sorry," I offered.

There was a pause on the other side. And then Peter's deep voice: "It's okay. I'm telling you, we'll find something on this disk."

We'd better.

THREAD FOURTEEN

———

The weather app said it would rain today. Not only rain, but storm. Despite the impending hurricane, my time in Florida had been accompanied by sunshine, heat, and humidity, showered by the occasional light drizzle. Although not the biggest fan of heavy rain's effect on my hair, I did, from time to time, miss the Costa Rican tropical deluges. So I was sort of looking forward to a night of reading to the sound of rain.

The afternoon air was light and chilly, so I decided to enjoy the last bit of it in one of the gazebos in Pembroke's gardens. It was a quaint, wooden structure varnished in creamy white paint, overlooking the brush that led to the ocean. Upon arriving, I learned if you stood up on the bench on your tiptoes, you could get a view of the tide line. In the gazebo itself though, you could only hear waves splashing rhythmically at a distance. A wooden bench went around the gazebo in a U-shape. It reminded me a little of the gazebo in *The Sound of Music*. Of Lisle's "I am Sixteen Going on Seventeen." Damn, she was young. I did a quick take to make sure no one was around. I placed my bag carefully on the ground, hoisted myself up on the bench, and began walking, skipping, and dancing in circles around it.

The romantic in me had been reborn after my conversation with Juliana yesterday. I loved her love story. It was so pure and simple, yet so seemingly unreachable in today's world. Such blind devotion to someone whose phone number you didn't have and whom you didn't know you could find… It was unimaginable. *Almost as unimaginable as what could have happened to her son.* Something was off. And now Peter had stumbled into this whole cornucopia, or maybe I should say Pandora's Box, of information. What should we be looking for in it?

Feeling a little breathless, I hopped off the bench and took a seat. The wooden benches, although beautiful in design, were not the most comfortable. I sat with my legs crossed over each other and my computer resting on my thighs. My head was still pounding a little from the skipping and the lack of sleep, but I was almost done with my Luciano article, and I wanted to type up what I learned yesterday.

I was making progress when my phone's screen glowed up with a message from Peter. I had saved his number now. *There is so much. Can I stop by in 15 min?*

Yes, I replied, and committed myself to typing non-stop in that time to drown my leaping thoughts.

* * *

For the first time since I began meeting Peter, his Jeep was not parked outside the gate waiting for me when I arrived. I paced back and forth for about five minutes, thinking about what my plan of attack for the information would be. Go over all the emails and scan the subject lines for something that stood out? No one would make the subject of an email *Secret Stuff* though. What about finding an infrequent sender?

Peter's Jeep pulled up soon after and he parked it and jumped out, all in one swift motion. His usual polo shirt and khaki pants were substituted by basketball shorts and a Fordham Soccer t-shirt. And, accordingly, his hair was a messy mat of brown, instead of being combed back as usual. I was tempted to tease him about how he looked, but I restrained myself and settled for, "Hi. So what do you have?"

"A lot and not a lot," Peter said, handing me a new envelope. "I started by looking at Dad's phone and email records of the two months before March 24, 2015. The day he disappeared."

"Okay, and…"

"It seems like he and Danny and a few other people were working on the stage-four clinical trials of a cholesterol pill. From the team emails, everything was ready for this pill to be launched into the market and they were just doing a few minor tweaks. There were some other emails from general HR company announcements and one or two with technicians about the instruments they were using. That's pretty much it in his emails."

"I see." I interlaced one hand over the other and rubbed my thumbs together thoughtfully.

"And then his phone and text records were mostly him speaking to my mom, Grandma, me, and a few college friends. The police also had these records because Lemirk couldn't cover them up as proprietary information. We were all interviewed a bunch. But none of us knew a thing. Most of us, except for Mom and Grandma, of course, were not even in Florida."

"So nothing?" I asked, feeling my right fingernails dig into my left hand.

"If I stopped there, probably. But I realized they had this work messaging platform at Lemirk to send quick messages to each other. Sort of like Skype. Dad was messaging Danny and his usual team, but also this guy Matt who hadn't come up in his emails or his texts."

"Okay." I felt my eyes widening in anticipation.

"Penelope, look at their conversation," he urged, opening up the envelope and shifting through its contents to pull out a stapled file and handing it to me.

He didn't let me read beyond:

February 20, 2015

Santiago- Hey

Matt- Hello

Santiago- How's it going?

Peter decided to snatch the file back and tell me the rest himself.

"So basically, their first conversation is about one month before Dad disappeared. Dad reached out and was like, 'I know yesterday when I ran into you at the lab after hours you said it was nothing. But I want to talk.'"

"Hmm."

"So the Matt guy is all like 'what about?' and basically Dad says Matt didn't work in that lab because it was the lab for human trials, so only human samples were processed there. And Matt was supposed to be working on an Alzheimer's pill that hadn't made it past pre-clinical trials because…"

"Because what?"

"The rats were dying. From accelerated heart rates, apparently."

"Wow." I could feel the air around us starting to cool down and the sky above become dotted with dark gray clouds.

"I know... so yeah, basically Dad calls him out for being there and the guy Matt brushes it off saying he was just borrowing some instruments." Peter started pacing back and forth on his side of the gate.

"And he was there after hours... that's so sketchy," I added. It was a bit odd, how we always stood there at the gate, but I was not about to be the one to suggest we go out somewhere. I was technically not allowed to leave either way.

"Right?" Peter asked, pausing his pacing to look straight at me. But it almost seemed like he was looking straight *past* me and into the nothingness.

"What else do we have on Matt?"

"Well, their next conversation is a few days later and it's Dad saying he saw the files that opened up in the computer at the lab and they had data about actual human trials."

"No way," I whispered, shivering as the temperature dropped even lower.

"Matt said there was nothing to worry about and those were just predictions."

"What the fuck? Is that all he said?"

"They keep going back and forth a few times with Dad saying he thinks something is off and Matt swearing it's nothing. The last message between them is two days before Dad disappeared. He said: 'We really do have to talk.' And that was it."

"Oh, my God, Peter that's so bad! If your dad found out this Matt guy was doing experiments without being allowed, then... he could have been the one who did it."

Peter nodded, looking out into space, his eyes blank. I couldn't imagine how he was feeling. He could've been reading the messages between his dad and his murderer.

"Did Santiago talk to anyone else about this?" I asked to break the silence.

"Not that I could see. I figured he'd tell Danny if anything, but he didn't."

"Hm." I began biting my right index fingernail before making myself stop. I went through a phase in high school where I bit my nails when I was anxious and the results were pretty terrible. "Did you find these records they were talking about? The ones of Matt's Alzheimer's pill on human trials? To have some actual evidence, you know?"

"I looked over hundreds of his Excel, Word, and Google Drive documents. I think he just saw them on the lab's computer as he said. So there's no saved version of them."

There was a silent pause, and I could hear the wind hissing as it brushed against the palm tree's sharp-edged leaves.

"Are there any emails from Santiago to himself?" I asked, breaking the silence.

"Are you saying…?"

"Well, when I'm writing and I find something important I want to use at the library's computer, I email it to myself," I explained, digging into the envelope Peter had handed to me and pulling out the papers with Santiago's email records. I scanned them quickly, guiding my eyes to those of February 19, which would've been the afternoon Santiago saw Matt at the lab.

And there, right on February 19, I found the line item for an untitled email from Santiago to himself at 6:17 p.m. It had one attachment.

"Genius." Peter shook his head in disbelief. "I wish we could just click on the paper and have it open up. I'll open it on my computer as soon as I get home."

"Yes, and send it to me, please."

"You got it," Peter said, letting out a deep sigh. "So what you just said about being at the library… you've always been a writer huh?"

"Yup. At least I've been trying to prove myself as one," I replied. Although I told myself to stay away from friendly conversation with Peter to avoid falling into a flirty joking banter as we sort of had before. I was never able to stick to this resolution when the time came.

"I began college as an English major," Peter shared, leaning against his side of the gate.

"Really?" I asked, with perhaps a little too much eagerness.

"Is it that surprising? You can't see me reading Fitzgerald and analyzing Poe?" His honey-brown eyes pierced intently into my own.

"I mean, whoever can't read Fitzgerald is someone I would rather not be friends with. I guess I just didn't see you as much of a sit-down-in-silence type of guy who spends hours analyzing the use of similes in a novel to advance the figure of a strong woman protagonist."

"What makes you think that?"

"Nothing specific." I was honestly not sure what it was about Peter that screamed more "action" and "adventure" instead of "reading" and "quiet."

"You're right though. The writing got me. I still loved the idea of dissecting each character and understanding them, but I didn't exactly want to write it all down. So I went into Marketing. Because customers are like characters, you know?"

"I hadn't thought of it that way, but I guess that could be true." I looked down at my nails. The nail polish had begun chipping. That bothered me a lot.

"I did this group project once that was super cool. My team and I had to go out and make recommendations for a local restaurant. I studied at Fordham, so my team got assigned a small pizza shop in the Bronx and we had to interview—"

"Shit," I interrupted when I began feeling some raindrops on my cheeks. "It's starting to rain." I silently cursed myself for not packing an umbrella with me, even if it was supposed to rain until later that night.

"Oh, come on, it's nothing." Peter laughed.

"It's supposed to storm tonight though," I countered, rubbing my arms. It was getting pretty cold.

"You call these little, innocent drops actual rain?" he asked as he, suddenly and without any warning, reached his arm through the gate's bars and began wiping the few raindrops that had landed on my cheek with his thumb.

I looked down at my feet so I wouldn't have to meet his gaze. So I could push away the stupid fantasy of both of us inching in, ever so close, as the drops started pouring down faster and harder until we were kissing in the rain.

The rain did pick up in the space of seconds and it started pouring. "Damn it," I said, reaching through the gate, yanking the remaining papers Peter was still holding in his hand, stuffing them into the envelope, and putting the envelope into my purse. "Gotta run."

"No, Penelope, you'll get drenched! Come into the car and wait it out," Peter insisted, grabbing onto my wrist.

For a second there, in the deafening, cold rain, it was only Peter and me. The rain had drowned out the entire world, and I desperately wanted to let myself give up and go into Peter's car. Let him take off his jacket and give it to me to warm up. Let him bend toward me and kiss me. But there was Ricky. I couldn't.

Thankfully, the coldness of the rain made me start shivering, and I shook my head in response. "It'll just get worse. I better get going."

"Wait," Peter said to my turned back. "Prove yourself to whom?"

"What?" I asked, feeling my hair getting heavy with water.

"You said you wanted to prove you were a writer. But who do you want to prove it to?" Peter asked solemnly, as if this question could not have waited a second more to be asked.

"Peter, I'm getting soaked," was all I could manage in response. And with that, I turned around and began running in the direction of the clubhouse before I resigned myself to walking; I was already completely covered in rain either way.

THREAD FIFTEEN

—

The day after it poured rain on me was cold, gray, and dreary. I resolved to spend it working in my apartment. No breaks or exercise or meals. I was punishing myself for not having written more than a few sentences yesterday. It also annoyed me I hadn't been able to stop thinking about texting Peter, mainly to find out what he'd discovered in the file Santiago emailed himself, I told myself. In reality, I couldn't stop thinking about Peter's question about whom I wanted to prove myself to. But all in all, I was mostly punishing myself for the kissing-Peter-in-the-rain fantasy.

When you get laid off, will your dumb ass want to lose your work permit and go back to Costa Rica forever or would you want to ask Ricky's mom or dad for a huge favor? An entire life of focusing on my academics couldn't amount to me "following my heart" now. It was all around unacceptable.

By 3:40 p.m. I was starving and couldn't focus on writing a single more word before I ate something or interacted with another human. Seeking human interaction in my phone would only result in me being forced to reply to Ricky's or my mom's texts, so I abandoned that thought. And since there was still an hour to go before dinner was served, I resorted to the tiny fridge in my room, which I had filled with snacks. It seemed like the day to bake the cookie dough I'd been saving. Thankfully, my apartment was equipped with a mini kitchenette, which included an oven. But after thrashing through all the cabinets in the apartment, frantically trying to find a stupid cookie tray, I gave up and collapsed on my couch to cry. I liked crying every now and then, releasing all that negative tension. However, I hated wallowing in self-pity for too long. So a few minutes later, I sprinkled some water on my face and resolved to find Juliana and ask to borrow her tray. I was even craving some time with her calming presence.

During one of our conversations, Juliana had mentioned she also lived at The Palms building in room 202. I had never been happier for my good memory than I was today. I went down the stairs, holding my cookie dough and my apartment keys in my hands, and knocked lightly at her door. When I heard no response, I knocked a little louder. I was about to knock again when the small, pale figure of a recently-bathed Juliana arrived at the door, wrapped in a fluffy white bathrobe with her hair still dripping wet.

"Can I... I have cookies," I said, raising the cookie dough package to her face in lieu of a greeting.

"God, Penelope, you made me run out of the shower!" Juliana replied, walking back in to sit on a chair at the kitchen table.

"I'm sorry, I didn't realize you were in the shower. Can I come in?" I asked, looking into her apartment for the first time. The walls were covered with framed pieces of embroidery. There was a big painting over her couch; from what I could tell, it was probably the work of Luciano. A single picture frame stood propped up against the wall on her kitchen counter.

"Yes, yes, come in," she replied, waving me over.

"Do you happen to have—"

"It's in the first cabinet. The top left one." That woman was really always one step ahead. "I've got a sweet tooth myself," she added with a wink, softening up and probably sympathizing with the frazzled version of me she was seeing.

Instantly, the sight of her sparkling green eyes and her dimples reassured me, and I felt safe with her. It felt like everything would be okay. Eventually.

I found the cookie sheet and some non-stick spray in the top left cabinet and got to placing my cookie dough on the sheet right away.

"It's been horrible, hasn't it?" I asked, pointing toward the window with my chin. It had been pouring rain steadily all day.

"My buttercups need some water." Juliana stared dreamily out the window. "I planted them in the back gardens where no one would notice. I don't think we're supposed to plant our own flowers. Plus, they're poisonous."

"What?" I asked, still standing in the kitchen waiting for the oven to finish preheating before being able to put the cookies in.

"Yes. Buttercups have some toxins in them that can cause dermatitis when humans touch them," Juliana explained. For some reason, this seemed to make her very happy.

"That's... unexpected." The oven was finally ready, and I popped the cookie tray in.

"It's always the ones you least expect, right?"

I was walking toward the kitchen table to take a seat next to Juliana when I singled into the lone picture on the kitchen counter. I could feel Juliana's eyes on me as I came closer to it, discerning the people in it.

It was a black and white picture of a beach. A young woman in her twenties was crouching on the sand so she could wrap her arms around the shoulders of two children. The boy to her left was wearing a hat, with the initials S.N. stitched onto it, and was looking slightly over his shoulder impatiently. The girl to her right was clutching some sort of toy in her hand and looked like she was about to cry. But the young woman, with dimples in her cheeks, smiling eyes, and long strands of chocolate hair that danced in the wind, seemed to be telepathically telling the kids it would all be alright.

"Those are some of my favorite memories," Juliana offered. "Rob and I would take the kids out to... it was a funny-named beach... oh, to Cherry Grove Beach on the weekends. We wanted to get away from the city. Rob's parents had a house out there so it worked out great."

"That sounds fun."

"Santiago loved the beach and swimming in the ocean. We could barely make him stand still for two minutes for Rob to take the freaking picture." She laughed. "And Caroline, well, she hated the sand. And the heat."

"Sounds a bit like my dad," I replied, making my way to sit with Juliana at the table. "I'm guessing the 'S' on his hat stands for Santiago. What about the N?"

"That would be 'Nadler,' his father's last name,'" Juliana explained. "In Brazil, some parents choose to make their kids' first last name of their mother. No one really knows why, but it's really up to the parents what last name they choose to pass on. I actually can't recall how Rob convinced me to give both the children his." Juliana shook her head, smiling. "I do remember when Santiago learned that was the convention in Brazil, he nearly decided to change his last name to mine.

That's how committed he was to making sure he and his sister would never forget where they came from."

"That's so funny, and noble you could say."

"I guess you're right, but it's also stubbornly righteous. Santiago always wanted to do what was right. I tried telling him there's not only one right answer, but he maintained you could always do 'the most right' thing. 'There's always one option that's a little more right than the rest,' he would insist."

I could see Juliana's eyes becoming glassy as she stared out the window, remembering her firstborn child. Her only son's words and his voice. I felt bad for having brought him up.

"Did Peter ever tell you about him?" Juliana asked, suddenly turning to face me.

"A little here and there," I said, shifting uncomfortably. Between the very weird, random questions I'd asked on behalf of Peter, I was sure she would put together what was going on. She either knew something was up and wasn't bothered by it or decided it was best to know as little as possible.

"Did Peter tell you about him as a living, breathing person?" she pressed on.

"Not really much, I guess," I replied, looking down at my lap.

"Do you want to hear the full story?" she asked, her voice solemn.

"You don't have to—"

"Do you want to, though?" Juliana insisted.

"Well… yes."

"He deserves to have it told," Juliana said resolutely, and she began the story of her son, which was, inevitably, also the story of his death. "Santiago married Ellie after they met at NYU…"

Juliana and Rob had also begun their married life in New York, but they had moved down to Florida when Rob retired. They were chasing the warm weather. Plus, Juliana's sisters wanted her to be a little closer to Brazil so that they could come visit. Santiago and Ellie had both lived all their lives in New York City. They pursued their professional careers for some time, then they got married, and they had the best of city life: young, successful, and in love. They were living a timeless dream. One that had been Juliana's, then Santiago's, and later on also became Peter's.

When Ellie got pregnant with their first child, they decided it was time to get away from the city and come down to Florida. Santiago started working in a lab for a big pharmaceutical company, Lemirk, doing what he loved the most: science experiments. And Ellie, with her background in Anthropology, also got a job at Lemirk in their Advertising department. So Peter grew up in Florida, happy and careless. Rob and Juliana took care of Peter often; after school before his parents picked him up, and whenever they were busy.

Rob died from a heart attack just before Peter finished high school. He was so close to his grandparents that Rob's death hit Peter really hard. Hence, as life would have it, Peter decided to go out to New York for college. He needed to leave to chase an ideal that few ever catch: that of a fresh start. Whatever that meant, anyway.

THREAD SIXTEEN

———

The timer on my phone, the one for the cookies I was baking, went off, but I just sat there, immobile. I placed my hand over Juliana's as she told her story, and I didn't want to let her go.

"Will you make me go get those cookies? God knows I need them," Juliana exclaimed, shaking her hands free from mine and pushing her chair to stand up.

By this point, she had walked me through the day when she first heard of Santiago going missing. Peter flew down to Florida. Juliana described how she, Peter, and Ellie wandered the city at night, pasting posters with Santiago's face on them. The searches they organized. Ellie's chilling shrieks. Peter storming off in tears. Her, sitting on the couch, clutching the sweater she had knitted for Santiago when he turned eighteen and went away to college.

"No, Juliana, let me; I'll get them," I said, bouncing up from my chair and pulling the tray from the oven. They looked perfect. I used a spatula to mount four warm cookies onto a plate and bring them to the table.

Without giving them even a minute to cool down, Juliana reached for one of the cookies and smiled as she bit into it. "It's hard, you know?" she mused, holding the other half of her cookie up in the air. "Losing Rob was very tough. But losing a son…" The cookie in her hand trembled a little.

"I'm really sorry," I replied, not knowing what else to say. I finally reached for my cookie, despite realizing I was no longer hungry.

"The day after they found his body, Ellie told me I had to move out. What she didn't tell me is she was having me committed to Pembroke," Juliana went on, biting into her cookie once her pulse steadied.

"That's awful."

"That's what I thought at first, but then… I don't know. I guess it ended up being good for me in the end. I would have been so alone in that house; it was the one in which Rob and I lived. There were all those memories of Rob and Santiago… It was good to get out."

"Good point."

"Ellie left their house too that same day. She didn't even tell Peter where she was going. Something inside of her finally snapped once she knew Santiago was gone. She never once contacted me again. I tried to reach her, but she wouldn't answer the phone. She barely picked up when Peter called. It was almost like he lost some version of her too."

I nodded sympathetically. There really wasn't much more I could do.

"Do you, um, do you want to go down for dinner?" I asked after we had been silent for over a minute. Looking out the window, I realized the sun was setting, which meant the dining hall wouldn't be open much longer, and I needed at least one meal.

"I don't know about you, but after those cookies, I'm anything but hungry." Juliana smiled softly.

"I think I could use some salad," I admitted. Skipping all meals today had finally caught up with me.

"It's settled, I'll head down with you. Let me just slip into some pants," Juliana said. She was still wrapped up in her white bathrobe.

* * *

I could feel my worn-down self reviving as I ingested real food; a salad, chicken breasts, and some rice.

The rest of the dining hall was nearly empty, except for two women sitting at a table way in the back. Juliana sat across from me with her fingers interlaced over each other, revealing her bright pink nails.

"So are you going to tell me why you really came to my apartment?" Juliana threw the question at me mid-chicken bite.

"I... the cookies," I said, a little taken aback.

"I've never seen you eat dessert," Juliana countered.

"I eat chocolates in my room all the time. And I do treat myself. Once in a while. Which is why I wanted to bake the cookies," I mumbled, looking down at my salad.

"I see." Juliana allowed a grin to creep into her delicate lips.

"If you must know, I hadn't really eaten anything else today before those cookies so I was really starving and had to eat them right then and there," I added, mounting the last bite of rice onto my fork with the help of my knife. "Eating like a lady," my grandma would say.

"Why didn't you eat anything before?"

"Um, the rain, you know? I didn't want to leave my room with all that rain."

Juliana just nodded, but she was doing that Juliana thing in which she simply looks at you and you want to tell her more.

"I was mad at myself. For, um, having thoughts I shouldn't have."

"Well now, Penelope, there are many things you shouldn't say or do. But your thoughts are yours and yours alone. Don't let anyone make you feel bad about them." This time, it was Juliana who put one of her hands on my forearm.

"Thanks, but... I just wish I didn't have the thoughts in the first place."

"I know exactly what you mean." Juliana really knew exactly what to say sometimes. "You know when I told you about how each person you meet has their own life of interwoven threads, and when you start interacting with them more your threads start intertwining with theirs?"

I nodded in response.

"You'll see your own thread is made up of individual fibers. And these fibers represent the relationship you have with yourself and your thoughts. Sometimes you'll meet people who will tug at your thread one way or the other, making you reevaluate what's inside of you. Or at the very least, look at it in a different way."

I nodded again, letting her words sink in.

"Does... does this have to do at all with the um..." Juliana began. I had never seen her struggling for words like this. Even as she told me the hardest story, of her son's death, once she was speaking, she just kept going. "With the pouch? The one you ran out to grab in your pajamas?" she finally finished.

Oh. My pouch. I liked to keep it physically close to me but mentally very far away.

"No," I said instinctively, but then, "I mean, not directly but—"

"Would you mind me asking...?"

I hadn't told anyone about the contents of my pouch. Not my friends, not my boyfriend. It was something that had happened in the past and I thought about from time to time, but not something that had to be discussed with anyone. And here was this woman, who I had known for less than a month, asking me to reveal its secrets.

"Dinner time is over," came a voice from the overhead speakers. "It's time for all residents to vacate the dining hall for cleanup."

Juliana and I both looked around and realized the dining room was, in fact, completely empty except for the two of us.

"Let's get out of here," I said, standing up. The interruption gave me a minute or two to decide how to respond to her request. Juliana followed my lead and we walked out of the sliding glass doors and into the equally empty hallway.

I was heading to the elevator and assuming we'd table this talk. We had, after all, been talking for over three hours by now. But Juliana was not one to let a time or place determine whether she could keep having a conversation. She lowered herself down against the hallway's cream-colored wall until she was sitting on the floor. She looked up at me with her gorgeous green eyes and patted the place next to her.

"Come on, we've got a conversation to finish," she said.

THREAD SEVENTEEN

—

Maybe it was the exhaustion of the whole day spent without food. Maybe it was the horrible weather still pounding with heavy raindrops outdoors. Or maybe it was the fact I couldn't talk about it, not now and not ever, with anyone else. It was Juliana or no one at all.

"Years ago, when I was still in high school," I began before even fully sitting down. "My mom, my dad, my sister Mariella, and I had gone out to dinner on a Friday night. We drove back home at around 9 p.m. My sister and I were sitting in the back seat, looking at our phones, and our parents were talking about some friend of theirs who wanted to open a bakery. And then, completely out of nowhere, we hit something. I remember I was Snapchatting a friend, and my picture was all blurry."

"Oh, my."

"What was that?" Mariella asked wide-eyed as dad pulled the car over to the side of the road. She was clutching her seat belt with one hand and her phone with the other.

"A dog probably..." I offered. "Right?"

"It sounded bigger," she gulped.

"A cow then," I said, biting my inner cheek. We lived in a rural area, it could surely be a cow. I hoped it was not too badly hurt.

Mom and Dad were silent. Then, without saying a word, Dad stepped out of the car. Mom turned to face us. "Stay in the car, girls," she said, before following him out.

Mariella and I exchanged confused looks. She began opening her side of the door quietly.

"What are you—"

"Shh," she cut me off, hopping out of the car and motioning for me to follow her.

"Rodrigo, do something," Mom shrieked. "He's not moving!"

"Natalia, what do you want me to do? He's dead. There's no pulse." When I stepped out of the car, I could barely make out Dad's outline, kneeling on the ground next to a crumpled bundle. But it was too dark to see much from where Mariella and I stood on the other side of the road.

"Should I call 911?" Mom asked, pacing back and forth.

"You know they won't get here for another hour. There's no use." Dad was still kneeling on the ground.

"So what do we do?" Mom quavered.

Dad was silent again. Mariella began tiptoeing her way to the other side of the street. I was going to scream out at her to stop, but I was as curious as she was; we had to see the horror with our own eyes.

Under the hazy, yellow light of the streetlamp, I began discerning the figure of a brown-skinned man drenched in dark violet. The night air carried *a distinctive, foul, metallic note: blood. The figure laying on the ground was wearing a plaid shirt we all would've recognized anywhere. The figure was, no doubt, Enrique; our property's watchman.*

Mariella stood there in silent shock. I felt like I was about to throw up. I don't know exactly why, but I pulled out my phone, which was open on Snapchat, and took a video of the scene.

"What are you doing here?" Mom turned to us, horror in her eyes.

"Penelope, Mariella," Dad said stoically, "Don't make me repeat this: get in the car. Natalia, go in too, and open the trunk."

We all stood there, mute and motionless.

"Now," Dad commanded with a firmness I had never before heard in his voice.

"You heard him," Mom said, wrapping her arms around our shoulders and urging us on, toward the car.

"Oh, and Penelope," Dad added, as we began making our way back to the car. "You better hope to God I don't find that video in your phone. Destroy it."

Juliana nodded attentively as I told my story, making me feel like it was okay to continue. She listened without interrupting, only letting out the occasional sympathetic sigh.

"So that was that. We live in a big, rural property so Dad just buried Enrique's body out there somewhere. And I showed him I erased the video from my phone. But, one year after, a copy of it showed up in my Snap memories and I... I don't know. I just couldn't erase the one last image I had captured of Enrique. It just didn't seem fair."

"So that's what you saved on—"

"Yes. It's what's on the flash drive I carry in my pouch. No one knows I kept it. And we never talked about any of it again, the four of us. We kind of just pretend it never happened," I concluded.

"That's a lot to keep inside, Penelope, and a lot to process. Didn't you all do something about it? And didn't you speak about it with anyone?" Juliana wondered.

"Well, I did bring it up to Mom once about a month after it happened."

"Do you know what ended up happening, Mom?"

"It was so dark and he was leaving his shift later than he usually would... And you know the road is so narrow there's barely any space to—"

"I mean," I interrupted, "what happened after we hit him?" Killed him.

"Your dad buried his body out there by the river," Mom stated matter-of-factly, her eyes on the road. I was driving and she was sitting next to me.

"But like, you didn't tell anyone? What about his family?"

"Penelope, they're all from Guatemala. He was an illegal immigrant. Your dad would've gone to prison for the rest of his life... And all for what?" She stared ahead at the blue mountains lining the horizon ahead of us.

"What about his kids in Guatemala who never heard back from him?" I asked. I couldn't help myself.

"It's just better this way."

I left it at that.

* * *

I made my way up to my room after dinner with Juliana, rubbing my arms with my hands to keep warm in the cool, earthy, post-storm night air.

Telling Juliana something from my past I hadn't told anyone else about was liberating. It's as if, in her spinning threads metaphor, intertwining your thread with someone else by telling them what's buried in your past takes off some of the weight of carrying that thread all on your own. It inspired me, in a weird way, to channel all of the anger I had toward my dad for doing what he did and my mom for not doing much about it, and using it to help shed light on a different truth. A truth that would bring peace to Juliana, to Peter, to Santiago.

To prove to myself I was committed to helping Peter and Juliana, and to shake off the uneasiness I felt after Peter and I's latest interaction, I decided to call him right then and there to ask him about the latest lead in our investigation.

Peter picked up after the first ring.

"Hi, Peter," I said as I fumbled around with my keys to open up my apartment.

"Hi, Penelope, how's it going?"

"It's alright, you know? I just, um, I actually just came from having dinner with Juliana."

"That's great. I hope you hugged her for me."

"I'm not much of a hugger," I said, letting myself melt into the couch.

"Watch out for when I see you next." He laughed.

"Noted." I felt a smile creeping up my lips and decided to change the topic quickly. "So did you find something?"

"What something?"

"Remember you said you'd look into that file in the email Santiago sent to himself with what he found in Matt's computer?"

"Oh."

"Yeah… did you?"

"Yes."

"And…?" Peter wasn't one to respond in monosyllables, and I didn't usually have to dig information out of him, so I was somewhat confused as to what he could be thinking.

"It's… I read the file."

"Good. Tell me about it! Are you bringing it over now? Maybe it's too late. Is it too late?"

"Penelope."

"What?"

"You can't tell Grandma about this."

"What do you m—I mean, of course, I won't tell her. But tell me. What is it?"

"It was some data on trials for that Alzheimer's pill… Human trials."

"Oh, shit," I said, bouncing off the couch and starting to pace back and forth in my apartment's living room. "The rats were dying, right? They really shouldn't test that on humans, it could be deadly."

"There were twenty-one subjects in the study, Penelope." Peter's voice was dropping lower each time he spoke, and he was freaking me out a little by the number of times he was saying my name.

"That's really bad."

"All of, um, all of their addresses were the same: 104 Pembroke Lane."

"Are you saying…?"

"Matt was experimenting on Pembroke's residents."

PART 3

THREAD EIGHTEEN

That following morning, I woke up exhausted. After a full day of not eating, spilling my personal secrets to Juliana during my first and only meal at 7 p.m., and finally talking with Peter—only to learn human trials were happening at Pembroke—I had not slept much.

Of course, that's when Ricky decided it was time to call. I really didn't feel like talking to him, but I figured ignoring him would only make things worse, so I picked up.

"Hi, Ricky," I said as his face materialized on my phone's screen in FaceTime. He seemed to be walking outside somewhere. I was still lying in bed.

"Loppy! It's so nice to see you, I miss you," he said, running a hand through his light brown curls. *He's very cute, without even trying.* He was wearing his stupid Cancun t-shirt from last Spring Break.

"I've missed you too, Ricky, it's been super stressful here with finishing up the story on Luciano and—"

"That's the painter you have to write about for work, right?"

"Yes, yes, that's him," I replied, propping a pillow behind my head to sit up a little.

"I'm sorry it's been stressful. And lonely too, probably."

"Mhm." I nodded, realizing I hadn't really felt lonely at all. "Do you just hang out with that old man?"

"Well, there's Juliana too." I started feeling a little restless, so I got out of bed to pace back and forth in the empty space in my bedroom.

"Cool, I didn't know you had friends close by. But aren't you like not allowed to leave that old people community now?"

"Yes. I mean, yes, I can't leave. Juliana's a resident here."

"Oh, I see… so she's not like a friend-friend, just like an old person friend," Ricky said, as his face was swallowed by a tree's shadow on screen.

"Um, yeah, I guess." I shrugged. The way he said that bothered me. Juliana might not be one of my college friend friends, but then again, I didn't tell my college friends what I told her. So who was truly my friend-friend in the end?

"Damn, Loppy, it's probably so boring down there. Are you ready to come up?"

"It's actually been fine," I said, getting more defensive because it really hadn't been boring at all, thanks to Juliana. And Peter, but I didn't want to mention Peter. Ricky was not really the jealous type, but I didn't need to give him a reason to be pestering me more about when I'd be done and ready to visit him at Duke.

"Oh." He sounded surprised. "Well, either way, it's much better up here. We're taking the boat out almost every weekend. My friends and I, you know? It's so fun, you'd love it."

"That does sound fun." I sighed, picturing my hair dancing in the wind as I sat on Ricky's frat's yacht, sailing the wide expanse of the lake with the sun warming the back of my neck. A part of me knew it would be fun to go there and live the lake house life.

"Well, you know…"

"I know. I just… you know I want to do this job right. I can't afford to screw up and—"

"I know," Ricky said, surprisingly understanding. "There's no stopping you when you get it in your head you're doing something."

I smiled a silent thank you at him for not fighting me on this and not making the day after my sleepless night more stressful.

"So what else have you guys been up to there?" I asked.

* * *

I subbed in for Mike at the guardhouse for about an hour after lunch as repayment. Then I was half wasting my time away and half roaming all around Pembroke to see if I caught sight of anything that seemed a little *off*. Of course, I was not expecting to see a crazy scientist walking around and discussing his experiments openly at the clubhouse's salon. It had been three years since Santiago found these documents saying experiments were going on. For all I knew, they stopped when Santiago talked to Matt. But the thriller-mystery-fanatic in me felt if I was alert enough, I'd see something. And the committed-to-help-find-out-the-truth in me wanted to find something helpful. So instead of taking a very much-needed nap, I took laps around the clubhouse and the gardens.

In one of those laps, I ran into Juliana, tending to some flowers. Her buttercups. When I first saw her, she was standing with both her hands on her hips, looking up into the blue Florida sky. I looked up too. There was something infinite about its complete blueness; not a cloud or anything else in sight, just blue. I noticed another vaguely familiar woman sitting on a chair next to Juliana, also staring off into space.

"Hi, Juliana," I said, handing her a little shovel she had begun to bend down to grab. "Here you go."

"Thanks," she replied, looking up at me with a look of momentary confusion. Then, "How's it going?"

"All good, you know. Haven't done much today."

"It's good to rest. You young people are always doing some sort of something." Juliana waved the little shovel in the air as she spoke.

"I guess we do," I said, looking at the other woman. She didn't seem to notice I was there or at least she didn't care in the least about my presence. Her white strands of hair were tied back in a long braid that snaked almost all the way down her back. I was finally able to place her: it was that woman I had spoken to when I heard the announcement about the hurricane over the loudspeakers.

"You know we tend to get busy to avoid thinking," Juliana continued. "It's definitely easier to occupy your mind with some task than to keep it still enough to focus on the important things."

I tilted my head to the side and looked up at the fat, yellow sun. "I do choose to do busy work whenever I want to avoid thinking about... stuff."

"Exactly." Juliana nodded, kneeling next to her flowers.

The other woman finally looked our way and smiled straight at Juliana without saying a word.

"By the way, this is my friend, Annie," Juliana offered, indicating with her head in the direction of the woman in the chair. "Annie," she began, raising her voice, "this is Penelope."

Annie smiled back at us without saying a thing.

"She doesn't..." Juliana began. "She can't..."

"I know," I said. I remembered she had brought up her clearly dead mom during our previous interaction. She was not mentally here.

Juliana nodded and got back to pulling out the weeds surrounding her buttercups. I looked down at my sundress and my exposed knees before kneeling next to Juliana and burying my hands in the soil to help her pull out weeds.

THREAD NINETEEN

———

I sat on one of the stools in the art studio, dangling my feet above the ground impatiently as I waited for my forest's dark green leaves to dry before I started adding the next layer of lighter green ones.

"Did you know I used to think we had one love and one love only?" Luciano threw this question out into the silent air. It had been a while since either of us had spoken, and I think he missed the sound of his voice.

"You did?" I asked. Our latest sessions had been focused a lot on his painting style and his sources of inspiration, so I welcomed this shift back to his life story.

After Marietta died from the miscarriage, Luciano was devastated. He thought that was it for him. He drove South to the Foresta Umbra, a forest on Italy's East Coast, with his baby Gloria. He was ready to drop off the face of the Earth and live quietly amongst the trees in mourning.

One day, as he was putting baby Gloria into a red and white striped dress that Marietta had bought for her, Luciano realized that—although different in

*nature than the love he had for Marietta—he had
so much love for Gloria too. He couldn't let her grow
up and know him only as a depressive recluse. So he
channeled all his pain and frustration into art. Soon,
he was back on the world's radar, and he and Gloria were traveling the world from exhibit, to private
showing, to conference, and back.*

Luciano waved his hands in the air grandly as he told
the story. He didn't even bother to put his paintbrush down,
and I felt a few drops of paint land on my cheek.

*Gloria became not just Luciano's travel partner
but also his friend and confidant. They were a team,
just the two of them. Then, during one of their trips
to an art show in New York, Luciano met Monica at
a cocktail party. She was, no doubt, one of the most
beautiful women Luciano had ever seen. Monica was
wearing a long red dress that wrapped tightly around
her gorgeously crafted figure. Her lips parted with a
mischievous smile as she descended the stairs in the
apartment's penthouse to join the rest of the guests.
Luciano soon learned that the beautiful woman was the
wife of the cocktail party's host. But that didn't stop him.*

*He talked with Monica all night and asked Gloria
to wait for him back in their hotel room. He didn't go
back to their room that night though. And after a few
coffee dates with Monica, Luciano told Gloria that
they were moving to New York.*

"Wow," I exclaimed in response. What else could I say?
My job, after all, was to take notes, not to comment.

"I know, a bit sudden, but you must remember I'm a romantic, Penelope. I knew I was falling in love, and nothing would stop me. Not even Gloria advising me against it."

"Not your daughter and not Monica's marriage..."

"Exactly!" Luciano said, apparently taking this as a compliment for his persistence. "A few weeks later, Monica and I got married at the Little Widow's Mite Baptist Church on Buhre and Westchester Avenue."

"I thought you mentioned something about being Catholic?" I wondered out loud aimlessly.

"Both Monica and I were Catholics."

I nodded, not really trusting myself to say anything in response to that.

"Anyway, it didn't work out with Monica either."

"I'm sorry." I was not.

"Wait, I said I'd show you this other painting technique while our oils dry," Luciano said.

"Yes, please do." I was ready to go back to art now.

"Okay," Luciano began, standing up and reaching for something in the supply bag he carried around with him everywhere. "Sometimes I want to zero in on a detail in my painting. So I have to make sure that detail looks very real." He turned over the five by seven sized piece of paper he pulled out from his bag, revealing a picture.

"I know you can look up pictures online, but there's something very powerful about going out there and taking a picture yourself. It gives you a much better sense of the spacing between objects, the angles, the colors... Here, take a look," he said, handing me the picture. "This is the one I used for a painting I started last month of a river at night."

I don't know what I thought the picture would be, but I was definitely not expecting to see what I did.

The picture was supposed to be featuring, I believe, the moon and the shadow it cast upon the water in one of the fountains in Pembroke's gardens. What I don't think it was supposed to feature was the guy in a white lab coat carrying a sort of kit under his arm. Lisa—yes, Lisa!—and two residents followed in tow, walking through Pembroke's dimly lit garden trails at night.

"What's up with that?" I asked, pointing at the little line of people on the picture's right-hand corner with urgency. "Is he a nurse? And why are they all out walking around at night?"

"No, no, the nurses' uniforms are blue. He's um... I think he's a friend of Lisa's? I see him around from time to time."

"When does he come? And what for?" I pressed on, my heart racing. Could Luciano really have captured someone doing more experiments on Pembroke's residents?

"I've seen him around at night a couple of times. I like to go for nightly walks once in a while to hear the sound of the crickets and the ocean. You know, it's also very important when you're a visual artist to be in touch with your other senses."

I couldn't care less about Luciano's art techniques right now, I just wanted a straight answer.

"But what are they doing out at night? Where are they going?"

"I... I don't really know," Luciano confessed, more so concerned with the fact he couldn't give me an answer than with whatever the hell was going on in the picture.

"I have to get going," I said, deciding I wouldn't be able to sit still through the rest of Luciano's lesson holding on to this gold-mine in my hands. "Do you mind if I borrow this?"

"No, no. Please take it, I don't need that picture anymore. But we were going to add the second varnish soon," Luciano complained.

"Would you mind doing that for my painting too?" I asked, knowing he couldn't resist the opportunity to say, if my piece turned out to be anything remotely close to good, it had been because of his expert guidance.

"I can do that."

"Thank you." I began walking out the door but stopped and spun on my heels to face Luciano and ask one last question he had to have an answer for. "When did you say you took this picture?"

"About a month ago?"

Holy shit.

THREAD TWENTY

——

"Holy shit," Peter said into the phone after I finished giving him the rundown of the picture I was holding in my hands. "Send me a picture of it."

"Okay, hold on."

"Wait, no. I'm coming over."

"Sounds good," I said. "I'll meet you by the gate."

By the time I got to the entrance gate, Peter's red Jeep was already parked outside and I was sweating drops.

"Wanna hop in?" Peter asked, sticking his head out the car's window. "I don't think I can stand out there in this heat."

"Sure," I said, making my way to Mike's guardhouse and asking him to let me out by promising, yet again, to sub in for him sometime next week.

I hopped into Peter's car, feeling a wave of icy, cold, air-conditioned air hit my sweaty self. I also realized it was only the second time ever I'd been inside his car. No bottles around this time thankfully.

"I can't believe Luciano had this," Peter said, taking the picture I handed him.

"I know. It's crazy," I agreed, wiping the film of sweat that had gathered on my upper lip with the back of my hand.

"So I can't really see all that well because the people are kinda small. But you see how the guy with the coat is wearing a blue cap with like a pinkish thing on it?" Peter asked, pointing at the guy's head.

I looked down at the picture again. The lab coat guy was giving his back to the camera, but his head was slightly tilted backward, as if he were checking on the rest of the group to make sure they were still behind him. After a minute of focusing on his figure, you could see a blue cap with a pink squiggly thing on his head.

"Yes."

Peter typed something into his phone quickly and held it up at me. "Doesn't it look like this?"

He was showing me the logo of a little angry shrimp holding onto an even tinier cutout of the state of Florida against a blue background. The search term read *Jacksonville Jumbo Shrimp*.

"What the hell?" I asked.

"I did some digging into Matt. He's originally from Jacksonville... that's the logo of their minor-league baseball team. It's like the only thing he posts about on Facebook."

"Oh, I see," I said. "So you think..."

"I think that's what's on his cap. It has to be him."

"So you think this means the, um, the experiments are still going on?" I asked, biting the inside of my cheek.

"You said Luciano took this picture a month ago, right?"

"Yup."

"I guess it does," Peter said, staring out into the blue Florida sky through his car's windshield.

"And I guess it means Lisa is somehow involved in all of this, right?"

"Wanna go get some ice cream?" Peter asked very suddenly, looking straight into my eyes.

His sudden pivot toward something as mundane as ice cream when we were in the middle of discussing our investigation surprised me. It was not like we really hung out aside from our meetings through Pembroke's gate's metal bars. What was even more surprising for me though was I usually got annoyed when someone distracted me from my work, which in this case was our investigation. Even so, I was not completely displeased by his changing topic.

"I shouldn't really leave Pembroke with the whole hurricane warning thing, you know," I managed to say, looking down at my hands.

We had gotten a few more warning messages and instructions on how an evacuation would work. It also seemed—we shouldn't get our hopes up too much though—the winds were pushing the storm east, off into the Atlantic Ocean and away from our coast. But things were changing every minute, so one couldn't be positive.

"It'll be quick. I know this great place that's super close by, and they have a killer raspberry sorbet."

"They really want to avoid us going in and out of Pembroke as much as possible, Peter... And what about the investigation?"

"Come on, Penelope, live a little! You know we'll be thinking about this investigation for the rest of the afternoon and into the night. We can take a break."

It was not the dimples that started peeking through his smile, not the temptation of a cold ice cream in this heat, but rather the realization I never really let myself do something just because it sounded fun that led me to roll my eyes and smile.

"Fine. But I have to be back—"

"Yes, yes. I'll have you back before sundown, Cinderella."

* * *

Peter parked right outside a quaint little pastel-colored ice cream shop called Downtown Ice. Inside, we were greeted by a solid blast of air conditioning and the sweet smell of sugar.

Being outside of Pembroke for the first time in a few weeks made me feel almost as if I had stepped into a dystopian, parallel universe. There were people of all ages, wearing all sorts of crazy outfits with a variety of vibrant hair colors; all of which were a huge contrast to the elderly population and blue-uniformed nurses I'd been living with.

"It smells amazing," I said, allowing myself to inhale it all.

"Hi, guys." The lady behind the counter greeted us. "There will be no sampling today, I'm sorry, we're running a little low."

"That's all right," Peter said, approaching the counter. "Give us two raspberry sorbets, please." Then, he looked back at me. "If that's good with you."

I nodded and rushed to the counter when I realized he was pulling out his card to pay for both of us. "Hold on. I've got mine."

"Don't be silly. I was the one who dragged you out here."

"Okay, I'll Venmo you."

"Penelope. It's really nothing," he said, handing me a light green cup with a big, fat scoop of raspberry pink sorbet in it.

I shook my head disapprovingly but decided not to fight him on it. Better not to make a big deal out of his having paid for me, right? We all knew this was most definitely *not* a date.

We began walking down the hexagonal-patterned sidewalk with shops and restaurants to our right and a grand avenue with a floral boulevard running down its center to our left. There were umbrellas—bright yellow, green, and blue—with patio chairs and matching tables lining the length of the sidewalk. Aside from the burning heat, the day was beautiful.

"I miss New York," Peter said, bringing a spoonful of sorbet to his mouth.

"What? During this gorgeous day?" I remarked, looking sideways at him in surprise. To think he could be thinking of that in the midst of such an amazing afternoon! I had even forgotten he used to live in New York during college.

"Don't get me wrong. I really do love Naples," Peter said, bringing another spoonful of sorbet to his mouth. "Don't *you* miss that boyfriend of yours up there?"

"No," I replied, a little too quickly. "I mean, he's not up there. He's at Duke," I said, somewhat taken aback by his bringing Ricky up. I had only mentioned Ricky once to him, and I often wondered if he remembered it at all. Apparently, he did.

"Oh, I didn't know that," Peter said, one of his eyebrows rising slightly. "I just... I miss the buzz of the city and its people."

"Interesting," I mused, glad we were switching topics. "You couldn't be wearing shorts in early March up there though." I swallowed a spoonful of sorbet and used the empty spoon to point at the navy blue cargo shorts Peter was wearing.

He gave me a dimpled smile. "Solid point. But there's something exhilarating about the way things don't ever stop up there. Does that sound weird?"

"I actually completely understand." I nodded, looking at the families around us. Children were visiting their grandparents, bouncing from side to side as they strolled leisurely down the street. Their eyes beamed with an airiness that comes with happiness and fulfillment. Had the family been walking down Park Avenue, you would've seen urgency and a sense of purpose shining through their darkened eyes.

"I'm glad I'm here now though," Peter shared.

"Me too. And it's really not as boring as I thought it would be with the whole investigation thing we have going on."

I let these words come out before really thinking about them and, once they were out, I realized it sounded like I was saying Peter's dad's death was a great source of entertainment for me. Why didn't I just shut up?

"Of course, it sucks though. Like, the reason why we're doing this in the first place really sucks," I added, to try to save myself.

Peter nodded. "Thanks for all your help." Then he slowed down, nearly to a stop, and placed his free hand awkwardly on my shoulder, "I wouldn't have gotten this far without you. Not a chance."

I smiled and took a step forward to get us moving again and not have to stare into his penetrating honey-brown eyes that could swallow you whole if you let yourself look at them too long.

"You're welcome. I'm thinking I'll start following Lisa around a little. To see what's up. I want to know when Matt's next visit will be to see if we can maybe…"

"Just be careful. Please," Peter pleaded softly. "Let me show you this super cool skating park nearby."

"You skate?" I grinned. "I had no idea."

"Just one of the many things you don't yet know about me," Peter said with a wink.

Yet.

THREAD TWENTY-ONE

———

I made a point of hanging out around the clubhouse the following few days, where I could get a view of Lisa coming in and out of her office. She was as cheery and smiley as ever. She really could've fooled anyone.

It was late on a Friday evening I saw the first sign of a not completely pulled together Lisa. I was sitting in a comfortable armchair on the very far left corner of the main salon, looking at my computer. I could say I was writing Luciano's article or starting some research on the retirement community industry for a follow-up piece Adrienne wanted me to write, but I was honestly just looking at pictures of illusion cakes that looked like other things on Pinterest.

The salon had been empty for a while and I think most residents had gone to bed, when I heard the tiniest sob coming from the main hallway. It was so small and fragile you could've mistaken it for the creak of an old door opening.

I closed my laptop gently and tiptoed quietly until I reached the main entrance. And there she was: Lisa crossing her thin arms over her chest and clutching onto herself. Her back was turned toward me, and she was standing in front of the announcements TV that hung right by Pembroke's main door. It sometimes showed a video tour of the community, taking visitors through its mini-golf course, its pool, and its gorgeous gardens. Sometimes it showed current residents in the salon playing board games or out walking on the beach. And sometimes it featured the picture of a resident, outlined by a delicate frame, and the words *"In memory of..."* right below their name.

Lisa was staring at the picture being featured *"In memory of"* a red-cheeked, white-braided-hair woman called Annie Dacier. I recognized her as Annie; the woman I saw in the gardens with her husband. Annie, Juliana's friend. I felt something inside of me sink. Something was unsettling about having seen someone alive and smiling not five days ago and now seeing her face here, frozen forever.

When I came back to it, I began approaching Lisa slowly. "Lisa?" I said, nearly whispering.

I think I startled her, for she gave a tiny jump and turned to face me. Her usual perfectly-made makeup was botched now; with black streams of mascara staining her porcelain cheeks.

She quickly wiped her eyes with the back of her hand and mustered a strained smile. "Penelope! You scared me!"

"Are you okay?" I asked, coming an inch closer. Although I knew she was working with Matt in some capacity, I still liked the woman. Who couldn't honestly? She was the nicest.

"Yes," she said, inhaling and exhaling deeply as she steadied herself. "Yes, it's alright. I just really liked Annie, you know?"

I nodded. "It must be hard. Growing attached to the residents only to see them... to not see them anymore."

"It is, it is," Lisa said, shaking her head. "And then you think: what about her dog? Annie had the cutest little golden

Cocker Spaniel. She's called Mimi. What will happen to Mimi now?" Lisa asked, and I could hear her voice breaking again.

"It's rough, I'm sorry," I said, putting my hand on her shaking shoulder.

"No, no, I'm sorry. I'm a mess. I'm sorry you had to see this." Lisa wiped meticulously at the new tears that had started flowing.

"No need to apologize," I reassured her. I figured she was sort of where I wanted her to be. I had to understand her vulnerabilities to figure out when and how I could get the information I needed from her.

"Thanks for understanding, Penelope. I appreciate it. I should probably get home though."

"Are you sure? We could go get some tea at the kitchen—"

"No. Thanks. It's alright. My husband will start wondering where I am and... It's better I go."

"Okay. Well, let me know if you need some company tomorrow or something. You know I'm around."

Lisa nodded and disappeared into her office, right off to the side of the main entrance. I stood there without moving for a minute, letting what had just happened sink in. A minute or so later, Lisa stepped out of her office, locked it, whispered, "Good night, Penelope," and walked out the main door.

Something about this whole interaction was bugging me. It was objectively pretty weird for Lisa to be standing in front of the monitor at night crying over a resident. Of course, she could grow closer to one resident or the other, but it still seemed odd for Lisa, who was always so put together, to be breaking down in the hallway. It was also pretty weird for a woman who is possibly aiding and abetting a crazy scientist to be feeling remorse over a death.

And then it hit me. What was really bothering me about the whole scene was I'd seen the full name "Annie Dacier" before and hadn't really connected all the dots. I'd seen it on the list Santiago emailed to himself. The one with the names of the subjects Matt was doing tests on.

THREAD TWENTY-TWO

———

Last night, after texting Peter about my potential discovery of poor Annie's connection to the trials, we strategized and decided the next step would be for me to go into Lisa's office and find the records of all the residents who had died in the past three years. In this quasi-detective roll I had taken on, nothing seemed more appropriate than sneaking in somewhere.

I camped out, yet again, at the clubhouse's main salon all day, sitting on one of the couches where, if I tilted enough to the left, I could see Lisa's office. So far, she'd walked in at 9:03 a.m. and spent all morning there, save for a two-minute bathroom break and a lunch break at 12:01 p.m. But she locked the office door and took the keys with her for that. As I gave Peter these constant updates via text, he offered to stop by the gates at around 3 p.m. to provide a "real" distraction: get her out of the office under the guise of a quick question he had to ask at the gate because he couldn't come in, and keep her out a little longer while I looked through.

My phone lit up with a text at 2:56 p.m.: *I'm almost there.*
Great, I texted back. Then I received a call. From Ricky.

I wanted to hang up and call him back later, but I didn't really know what to do with myself with all the adrenaline and anticipation rushing through me right now, so I picked up.

"Hey," I said, a little short of breath as my heart started beating faster.

"Hi, Loppy. Are you alright? You sound a bit... breathless?"

"Yes, yes, all is good," I replied, getting up to pace the salon and get a full view of Lisa's office.

"Okay. I'm glad. How's it going?"

"Oh, my god, she picked up the phone."

"What?"

"It's, um, a bit of a long story, I guess."

"I've got time."

I looked down at my phone and didn't see any texts from Peter. Lisa was still on the phone. So I figured I had a little under two minutes to catch Ricky up.

"So basically, do you remember Juliana?"

Silence. "Um..."

"It's fine. I'll just tell you. She's a resident here. And we've become friends. So I learned her son died a few years ago. And I met her grandson and he told me his dad was actually murdered and he's sort of investigating the murder. And now I'm kind of like helping him with the investigation."

"What the hell, Penelope?"

"What do you mean? I've always wanted to help solve a mystery. Juliana and her grandson deserve to know the truth."

"So you're staying down there in Florida to be some sort of rogue detective for a murder that happened years ago? You don't know shit about actual police and detective work. That's so stupid. You should've just come up here forever ago."

A part of me was shocked at Ricky's meanness and wanted to be hurt by his words. But another part of me had known, all along, he'd react this way if I ever told him about my involvement in the investigation. That part of me was almost glad this was his reaction.

I felt my phone vibrate and pulled it away from my ear to read the incoming text from Peter: *Here. About to ask the guard to get Lisa for me. Be ready.*

Got it, I typed back. Then I put the phone to my ear. "You know what?" I asked, oddly calm considering the whole situation. "You're right. I've been stupid."

"I'm just glad you—"

"I was stupid for thinking I could share this with you."

"What do you mean?" Ricky asked, his voice rising a little.

In the background, I saw Lisa starting to shuffle away from her desk.

"I have to go now."

"Wait, just—"

"I can't do this now," I said. And with that, I hung up and made my way closer to Lisa's office. She stepped out, did a double-take—perhaps thinking of the keys in her purse and the phone she was leaving on her desk—and stepped out, letting the door slip shut on its own.

As soon as Lisa stepped foot outside the clubhouse's main door, I sprinted up to her office and let myself in. My heart was beating so fast I could hear it pounding in my ears, but I willed myself to focus.

Just as my mind started worrying about her computer passcode, I took a breath of relief seeing the screen had not died down yet. Amazing.

I sat down on her tan, leather chair and started typing *"death certificates"* into the document search bar. A bunch of individual documents appeared on the screen, each labeled: *[Name] Death Certificate.* I plugged in my flash drive—I knew something good would come out of carrying it around constantly—and started loading the individual documents into it. Just in case. But I needed a spreadsheet of sorts with dates and details. What would that be called?

I tried *"Death records."* Nothing. *"Resident records."* A million different files that, from the ones I opened, contained apartment leasing information, dietary restrictions... I felt a layer of cold sweat starting to build up on my upper lip. What the hell would Lisa call this document?

My phone vibrated with Peter's text: *She'll be heading back soon.*

Shit.

I got up from the chair and started pacing. I glanced over the paintings and the framed pictures in Lisa's office, as if an answer would materialize across them.

Then my eyes landed on the corner of her desk where she stuck a few sticky notes, and I began scanning them frantically:

Call Mr. Evans about moving
Order more hand soap
Update Resident Status Log

Bingo.

I searched *"Resident Status Log,"* and a recently opened Excel file showed up. I saved it onto my flash drive without opening it, waiting the full twenty seconds before the computer announced, "file copied," and bolting out of Lisa's chair and her office. I was barely five feet outside the door when Lisa reentered through the clubhouse's main entrance with an air of annoyance and a brown bag in her hand.

"These kids think we're a delivery service or something," Lisa said into the air, to no one in particular. Then, directed more toward me, "Juliana's grandson wants me to give her this bag with her favorite dessert or something. That's not allowed, but I just couldn't say no to that smile… Have you met him?"

"Yes, I have," I said, my heart still racing and my hands shaking a little.

"Guess I'll get one of the kitchen staff to take it to her room. As if we were a delivery service," Lisa said again, shaking her head and going into her office.

GOT IT! I texted Peter. *At least, I hope I did*, I added on a second text, and no more than thirty seconds after, I was getting an incoming call from him.

"Penelope, I'm out here. Bring it to me!"

"On my way."

* * *

Sitting next to Peter in his car, I felt my stomach turn as we waited for the document to open up on his computer screen.

"What if—" I began.

"It's okay," Peter said, placing a hand lightly on my knee and quickly bringing it back to his computer's trackpad.

On the screen, a large Excel document with several tabs opened up. *Resident Info, Resident Contacts, Resident Deaths.*

Peter's mouse went to the Resident Deaths tab and there it was: a list with columns for each resident's name, the date of their death, the cause of death, and death arrangements.

"This is it," Peter whispered.

Minimizing this document, Peter opened up the one Santiago had emailed to himself with the names of the residents Matt had been doing tests on.

One by one, Peter typed up the names of the residents getting tested into the search bar at the top of the Resident Deaths tab. One by one, he highlighted in yellow the names of the residents who appeared in both spreadsheets. We were both completely silent as more and more rows turned yellow. Annie Darcier was the last.

"Eight," Peter finally said, looking over at me. "Eight out of the twenty-one subjects Matt is testing on have died."

THREAD TWENTY-THREE

———

"Holy shit," was all I could manage as a response to Peter's announcement eight out of the twenty-one test subjects had died. And under the *"Cause of Death"* column they all had the same item: "?"

"This is so fucked," Peter said, stepping out of the car and walking away. I thought he would just pace a little back and forth, but he just kept going.

"Wait, Peter!" I screamed, confused. This was definitely a lot to process, but Peter usually just kind of kept it together. Where was he going? He'd left his keys here and everything.

When he didn't stop walking and didn't turn back after I called out to him, I scrambled to turn off the car and jumped out of it too. Peter was now barely in sight, walking a couple hundred feet ahead of me.

"Peter!" I yelled again. When I got no response, I began jogging a little, making up for enough distance to see him take a right into the Pembroke mini-golf field.

When I finally made it there, I realized the whole field was fenced off. The only thing he could have done to get in was climb the metal fence and jump in.

I took a deep breath as I considered my options and, deciding if he straight up ignored me, he wouldn't pick up his phone either, I prepared to jump the fence too. I struggled a little hoisting myself up with both hands and fumbling around with my feet to find something solid to push myself off. I kind of managed to do so and, without thinking much about what would happen next, powered myself over the fence.

I landed on the other side on my right knee and elbow, whispering, "Shit," under my breath. Thankfully, the turf softened the blow and I barely scraped my knee. Dusting myself off, I got back on my feet and looked around the empty field.

I was not really into golfing or mini-golfing, and I had only been here once before when Lisa gave me the full tour of the property. The course itself was pretty cool, with tiny fake waterfalls, hanging bridges, and palm trees scattered everywhere. I scanned the field for signs of Peter's blue polo shirt but saw nothing. Finally, my eyes zeroed in on the figure at the top of a fake rock structure with two tall pillars and, in between them, a wall of falling water.

I sighed as I made my way to the rock structure and prepared myself for more climbing. When I finally joined Peter at the top, he was staring off into the empty blue sky and didn't acknowledge me.

I sat there silently for a minute and tried, "So... that was a lot to take in."

Silence.

"It all really sucks, Peter. I'm so sorry." With this, I placed my hand on his shoulder.

He turned to face me, stared into my eyes, and neither of us said anything for what felt like forever.

Then, still looking straight at me, he said, "Thanks for being here with me, Penelope."

I felt warm on the inside and had to look away. "Of course." And then, to lighten the mood, I said, "You're aware I could've driven away in your car and stolen it if I wanted to."

"You could have!" Peter's dimples started materializing themselves on his cheeks. "It's real nice of you to not have done that."

"I know."

"Should we play mini-golf?" The afternoon sun's rays bounced off his brown eyes and lit them up with the question.

"Well, I don't really—"

"It doesn't matter. It's just for fun," he said, jumping off the six-foot-high rock structure and holding out a hand for me. "Come on."

"Oh, I'm not jumping off like that," I declared, shaking my head.

"It's really not high at all." He smiled.

"Peter, I—"

"Grab my hand. I swear I'll catch you."

"But I can just climb down—"

"Come on, Penelope!" There it was again, something in the excitement in his voice, something about the way I knew he would make sure I was safe made me roll my eyes and take a deep breath.

"Fine," I caved, reaching my hand out to grab his.

"One..." Peter began. "Two..."

"Three!" I said and jumped off the rock into Peter's arms.

He stumbled a little and lost his footing, tripping into the cascade of water beneath the rock pillars and falling into the water.

"Oh, my god," I laughed. "I'm sorry you—"

"I'm not going down alone," he said, pulling me with the hand he still had a hold of and dragging me into the water too.

The whole scene was so rom-com-ish I almost wanted to laugh out loud and play into it like a character in a movie. But before I let myself fall for it all, I stepped out of the water, shaking my head and my whole body to get the water off.

"I can't believe you just did that to me," I chuckled, wiping water off my arms and legs.

Peter, still standing in the water, only smiled. "You have to admit it felt good in this crazy heat."

I wanted to say something snarky back at him, but he was right; it did feel good.

* * *

I could feel myself smiling on my way back to Pembroke after my little adventure on the mini-golf course with Peter. As if on cue, my phone started vibrating with an incoming call from Ricky.

After our last call when I was about to sneak into Lisa's office, I knew we'd have to have "a talk." Might as well have it now that I was feeling good.

"Hello."

"I wanted to make sure we're good after that call earlier," Ricky began, getting straight to the point.

"I... yes. Don't worry," I said, deciding it was not worth a fight.

"Awesome. Because I actually have an idea."

"What's that?" I asked, kicking a stone that was laying in the middle of the road.

"Some of the guys and I are renting a cabin in the mountains for the weekend," he began.

"Okay," I prompted, already knowing where he was going with this.

"So I was thinking maybe you could come meet me here, and we could go there together? There will be other girls too. Actually, Molly's going. You like her, right?"

I know Ricky had the best of intentions here and was trying to make things work, but I was probably not completely over how rude he'd been before. Something sort of went off in me, and I didn't want to stop myself.

"So you'd rather plan a weekend trip with the bros than come down here and visit me?"

"Well, I was thinking you could meet me—"

"I heard that. But you wouldn't think of coming down here, would you?"

"I mean, you're not really doing anything down there. You said you're basically done with your work story—"

"You really don't listen to anything I say." I stopped my pacing and sat on the grass off to the side of the road to keep myself from feeling shaky.

"What do you mean?"

"I told you I was helping out my friend Juliana—"

"The old woman? She's your friend?"

"Yes, she's my fucking friend, Ricky!" I snapped, feeling my patience run out.

"I just don't get it, Loppy."

"You don't," I said, and I suddenly felt myself smiling. That was it; he didn't get why I wanted to stay, and he never would. I know he heard what I was saying, but he never really bothered to *listen* to it. Or understand, for that matter. "I think it's better we just acknowledge this won't work."

"Wait, what?" Ricky's usually deep, cool voice raised as high as I'd ever heard it go.

"Yes, Ricky. You don't really bother to listen or understand me, and I don't bother to do the same for you. And it's fine. I don't hate you for it."

"Where is this even coming from?"

"I don't know, I just... Juliana's like my only friend here, and I've mentioned her a couple of times and you don't even remember her. But it's fine, it really is. It's best we just end things."

"This is bullshit."

I felt oddly even-tempered, almost relieved, as I let Ricky go.

"It's really not, Ricky, you know it's not."

"This is like so out of nowhere, Penelope... Honestly, what the fuck?"

"Take care, Ricky," I said into the phone. I hung up, got up from the curbside, and walked back into Pembroke's clubhouse.

* * *

I had a feeling of lightness in me as I walked into the main salon; a feeling that only got better when I saw Juliana, sitting in a corner, stitching something.

"Juliana!" I exclaimed.

"Hello," she said, looking up and smiling with her shining eyes. "I haven't seen you in a few days, have I?"

I was not purposefully avoiding Juliana, of course, but you could say I was not actively seeking her out either. With the investigation hitting too close to home in Pembroke and knowing she'd been friends with Annie, I almost feared she'd bring something up and I wouldn't be able to hide everything I promised Peter I would.

I went for a simple, "I know," and took a seat on a couch across from the one she was sitting on.

"Are you okay?" She pointed at the scrape on my leg. The one I got when breaking into the mini-golf course about an hour ago.

"Oh, that," I said, looking down at it and smiling at the recent memory. "You can blame your grandson for that."

Juliana opened her eyes a little wildly and raised her eyebrows. "Do tell, please."

"We just hung out," I mumbled, looking down to avoid eye contact, in case Juliana could see in my eyes the real reason we were hanging out.

"I see." She smiled and looked back down at her stitching. From where I sat, it looked like a golden, yellow circle suspended in mid patch. Where had the other flowers disappeared to?

"Yup." I nodded and, as it usually happens with Juliana, I felt the need to add even more when she was not asking for it. "I broke up with Ricky. Literally just now."

She stopped stitching for a moment and was silent. Then, looking up to meet my eyes, she said, "You look good—actually more than good—you look happy to me."

"I am."

"Then I'm happy for you too," she pronounced, reaching over to give my arm a squeeze and going back to stitching. The yellow circle began growing what seemed like yellow limbs on one of its sides.

"I knew Ricky and I just… I guess we just focused on different things. And I didn't feel that excitement and anticipation when he called anymore, you know?"

Juliana nodded.

"I think I even dreaded having to talk to him. He would just never understand."

"If you can't share the stories of your life with the person you allegedly love, your threads just stop intertwining. And there's not really much to fight for. You know?"

I nodded. Her thread metaphor was really growing on me.

"There's something else though," I began, and I couldn't believe I was going to say this out loud because I hadn't even admitted it to myself. "There might have been some other, um, subliminal reason why I wanted to end things."

"What's that?" Juliana asked, looking up from her stitching again.

"I think I sort of… It's not that I like…" I began, looking down at my hands as I clenched and unclenched them.

"I know you do," Juliana said with her ever-so-comforting dimpled smile.

"Do what?"

"Like Peter. In some way."

"I haven't even fully let myself admit it but… I think I do."

"I see it. In the way your eyes shine a little when we bring him up."

"They do that?" I asked, instinctively bringing my hand up to the side of my eye and brushing my eyelashes.

"You know he does too, don't you?"

I could feel my heart beating more quickly in my chest. I'd felt some signs from Peter, I was not dumb, but I'd been avoiding all these thoughts and feelings while I was still with Ricky, so I just chose to ignore them.

"Does what?" was all I could manage to ask.

"Like you."

Sitting in the cold air-conditioned room of the clubhouse in my still-damp clothes, I felt warm.

THREAD TWENTY-FOUR

———

Excitement filled the air at Pembroke. Flowers were being carried one way, tent pieces being pushed the other. There was talk of bells and vows, talk of a priest coming for the ceremony.

Lucy and Liam, two Pembroke residents, were getting married. Lucy was seventy-eight, Liam eighty-five. Neither of them had been married before. Liam had had a life partner who'd passed away years ago, and Lucy had had a daughter with one of her lovers in her youth. She never even bothered to tell him she was pregnant.

Upon hearing about the wedding from Juliana and hearing Lucy and Liam wouldn't wait for the hurricane to fully pass before officiating it, I volunteered to go out and buy a dress for Lucy. I got her measurements—5'3", size 4—and a general feel for her style; old-fashioned, simple, with lace finishes. With that, I set off to a small boutique store in Ron's van, making him promise Lisa would not hear a thing about my little outing in the name of love.

"Hello! Welcome, Miss." The woman at the entrance of the boutique looked down at the notepad where she presumably wrote down all the appointments. "Miss Penelope. We have you here for 3 p.m., come on in! I take it you came here alone?"

I had normally explained myself by getting into how the dress was not for me and how, yes, technically I was alone, but it was more of an errand. That day I settled for a "Yes."

* * *

Two days after, Lucy and Liam got married under a white tent on the beach; the sound of the waves replaced the orchestra, which was told they could not come in because of the risk of having more people at Pembroke in case of a last-minute evacuation.

"Hurricanes make no exceptions," Lisa replied when Juliana pulled her to the side to ask her to make an exception, just this once, for the orchestra to be allowed in.

Peter, on the other hand, had slipped past Lisa's scrutiny and was now sitting on a plastic chair in the same row as Juliana, Luciano, and I. Earlier this morning, after Juliana and I fitted Lucy into her dress and were starting on her hair and makeup, Luciano came to us in a flutter about Liam's suit being a mess. Luciano, ever the fashion and style freak, insisted we get Liam a new suit before the wedding. Juliana swooped in, offering to ask Peter to get it, and by the time she and I were putting a shade of light pink lipstick on Lucy's thin lips, Peter had snuck in through the beach and delivered the suit to Luciano and Liam.

After the priest's, "You may now kiss the bride," all the residents exploded into their version of screaming and jumping, which was a lot of soft clapping and tear-shedding.

Taking advantage of the momentary commotion, Peter leaned in and whispered in my ear, "Find me off to the side by the bushes when this ends. I've got something. It's big."

I nodded silently and felt the hairs on the nape of my neck prickle.

"I think I'll get going now," Peter told Juliana, Luciano, and I after about half an hour. We were all gathered in a little circle off to the right of the tent. There was no reception or dinner after this wedding, so we were all just standing around for a while. I had chosen the spot that faced the ocean to allow my gaze to get lost in its rhythmic, turquoise waves.

A few minutes later, I also excused myself saying I had some reading to catch up on for work.

"You go do that reading." Juliana grinned, giving me the tiniest wink. And somehow—like she always did—Juliana knew where I was going.

As I walked away, I looked down at my phone to figure out where, in fact, I was supposed to be going.

Walk out a little and then turn to your right. I'm by the bushes there, read Peter's message.

On my way, I texted back.

Sure enough, he was there, sitting on the wooden border that separated the soil and the bushes from the sand and the ocean. It was a little past 7 p.m. and the sky's painter was beginning to add layers of faint pink and orange to the canvas.

"I'm excited," I said, in an attempt to get Peter out of his sky-staring trance and announce my arrival. "And nervous too, I guess."

"Come over." Peter motioned, patting the wooden border next to him, his eyes sparkling through his long lashes.

I took a seat, keeping about a foot between us, and watched in silence as he pulled out his phone and pressed "play" on a video.

It showed what seemed like the entrance to a big, white building with the words *Lemirk* over a pair of gigantic, slid-ing glass doors. A few seconds in, a man stepped out of the building. I didn't recognize him immediately, but doing a mental inventory, I assumed he was Santiago. Right after him, a woman, dressed in an all-white suit, followed him out. I did recognize her: it was Lisa. My eyes floated to the top right corner of the video and read the time stamp: 12:09 p.m. May 24, 2017. The day he disappeared.

"Holy shit," I gasped, looking up at Peter.

Peter nodded and I could see the pain in his eyes. But even stronger than the pain was a ferocity, an anger, a resolution to get to the bottom of this.

"I was able to get the lady at the police department to give me a few of the Lemirk security videos from around that time. I asked her a while ago but they were part of the classified stuff Lemirk's lawyers won't let the police see. Apparently, the police had ordered the security guys at Lemirk to give them the tapes, and they had; but as soon as the police were about to start watching them, the lawyers stormed in and collected all the tapes back. My friend at the police department said everyone thought the lawyers had taken everything, but when she went to the file closet under the request of one of the officers a few days ago, she found a few unlabeled tapes and... Anyway, there's really nothing on the other tapes, but this is from the day he disappeared. And remember how no one saw him after lunch?"

"Mhm."

"Well, Lisa did. She has to know. She…" Peter's voice trailed off, the thought hanging heavy in the sticky, salty sea air. The sky's painter was going for stronger hues now—hot pink, bright orange, and yellow—with streaks of gold outlining the few remaining clouds.

"Do you think…?" I couldn't help myself from blurting the question out loud.

"It could've been her," Peter stated, turning to face me. His figure, now hiding in shadows, was outlined by the sun setting behind him. There was something chilling about the thought he'd just sat through a whole wedding a few feet away from someone who could've been responsible for something that hurt him so much. Something that changed his life forever, something he'd never get over.

"What do we do about this?" I whispered, as if not ready to hear his answer myself.

"I think we show her this. The video. You said she was already crying about that resident who passed away—Annie, right?—so maybe guilt is catching up with her."

"So we don't go to the police?"

"And have the lawyers discredit every piece of our story because of how we came upon this video?" Peter shook his head.

"You're right."

"I think we show it to her, see how she responds, and go from there."

"And record the conversation, of course," I added.

"Exactly."

"Should we try to find her now? She might still be—"

Peter shook his head gently, staring off into the horizon. "Let's just let a wedding be a wedding. All about happiness and love. Can we just let it be pure and simple like that?" Peter asked, almost pleaded, as he turned to face me.

I nodded. "Yes. Yes, of course, we can." And then, without thinking much of it, I inched a little closer to him and placed my hand on his knee. Instead of the usual wave of guilt and alarm I felt before whenever our hands or knees touched, this time I just felt warm and tingly.

In one swift movement, Peter pushed himself closer to me, grabbed me by the neck, and kissed me. At first, a soft, gentle kiss, then stronger and faster as his hands began going up my hair and down my back. Then he stopped, pulled away, and looked at me with his gorgeous smile.

"I've wanted to do that for... I think since the first time I met you," he confessed. The sun had dipped into the sea, and I could only see his shadow now. I think his eyes were sparkling.

"I... me too," I admitted, looking down at my hands. The night breeze was beginning to blow. I suddenly felt chilly, so I wrapped my arms around myself for warmth.

"But wait, how did you know to do it now?" I asked, tilting my head a little to the right.

"I heard about the, um, the break up," Peter revealed, looking down.

"I'm glad she told you," I said, letting myself stare into his eyes and leaning in again.

"You know what you taste like?" Peter asked before we kissed again, our faces inches away.

"Oh, no, do I want to know?"

"Caramel," he said. Then he leaned in and we started kissing again, making me forget the cold night air.

THREAD TWENTY-FIVE

———

At the beach, Peter and I decided we'd talk to Lisa the next day. What we didn't decide was what exactly our kiss meant. Would it happen again? Would he bring it up? Would I?

These thoughts were still running through my head when I walked into the clubhouse the following afternoon and saw Peter sitting on a chair in the far right corner, looking down at what seemed like a magazine.

"I see you've made yourself comfortable," I said as I approached.

"Yes, indeed I have," he agreed, looking up at me with his smiling brown eyes.

"Do I even want to know how you snuck in?"

"The mini golf, of course," Peter declared, standing up and putting the magazine back down on the table and revealing its cover. It featured a beautiful young woman with sharp cheekbones, a white dress, and the red words *Vanity Fair* sprawled behind her.

"Quality reading material," I joked, pointing at the magazine.

"I was trying to blend in, you know?"

"A white wig would've been better." With that, his dimples appeared. "Anyway, let's do this."

"Yes." Peter nodded. "I have the video here on my phone. So I think we just knock at her door and show her this when we get in."

"And then?" I asked, as we began walking toward Lisa's office.

"I'm not really sure," Peter confessed, without slowing down.

A minute later, Peter was knocking at Lisa's door. Through the glass window of her office, I could see she was at her computer, not looking particularly busy or idle. She looked a bit taken aback upon hearing the knock and seeing Peter through the window, but regardless, she opened her door and greeted us at the doorway.

"Hello, nice to see you!" she began in her cheery voice, "I'd love to invite you in but we're really not supposed to have visitors and I'm busy right now with—"

"You'll want to see this," Peter interrupted, bringing his phone up.

"What do you mean?" Lisa's smiling mouth and eyes dropped.

Without further explanation, Peter pushed his way into Lisa's office and I followed.

"I think you'll want to take a seat." He directed, pointing at her desk chair.

Lisa looked at me, her eyes growing big with concern. "Penelope? What's going on?"

"Just... just sit," I said, starting to feel my stomach knotting up. This was it. Soon we'd have some answers.

When Lisa sat down, Peter held his phone right in front of her and pressed play on the video. I was standing across from them, so I was not looking at the screen, but I recognized the sound of the automatic doors opening once for Santiago, then starting to close up but popping back open for the second person who was walking behind him: Lisa.

"Look at the date," Peter ordered, still holding the phone to Lisa's face. His voice was steady and unwavering, and I'd never seen him be this serious. Even I was a little scared.

Lisa sat still, hugging both her arms and curling into herself.

"This was the day he disappeared," Peter went on, slamming the phone down on the desk. "The last time anyone saw him."

Looking down at the floor, Lisa began shaking her head.

"You were with him that day. At that time," Peter pressed.

Lisa was still staring at the floor, but I could see her eyes had turned watery.

"What did you do to him, huh? Tell me, Lisa, what did you do?" Peter asked, dropping on one knee so he could glare straight into Lisa's face.

"Nothing," Lisa whimpered, barely audible.

"Nothing? So you're the last person to have seen my dad alive and you know nothing about what happened to him?"

"Peter..." I said, not really knowing what else to do. I wanted her to respond just as badly as he did, but terrorizing the already terrorized woman didn't seem like the most effective method to me.

"We have a picture too," Peter pressed on. He stood up from his kneeling position next to Lisa and began pacing back and forth. "It shows you walking around in the gardens at night with that Matt guy and the residents he's testing on. You know what? I bet the woman who died... Annie, right? I bet we could identify her on the picture."

"How did you get—" Lisa began.

"That's what you ask now?" Peter cut her off. "I can't believe you'd have the nerve after what you've done. Or what you've allowed to be done to so many people."

With that, Lisa began shaking her head again more frantically. "I really liked Annie, I would never—"

"Then what happened?" Peter demanded.

Wiping the stream of tears that had now poured down her cheeks, Lisa's blue eyes met Peter's. "I'll tell you."

Peter nodded, stopped his pacing, and folded his hands over his chest expectantly.

> Four years ago, Lisa and Jim had just gotten married, but they were going through somewhat of a rough patch financially. Jim got in an RRV accident on their honeymoon trip to Lake Tahoe, so he was out of work for a while. He started taking an extra painkiller because his leg hurt. And because he could. Then it was two extra pills per day and then five. Soon, Lisa was paying for Jim's rehab. With him out of a job and Lisa working extra hours despite being five months pregnant, she was getting pretty desperate.

I nodded at Lisa encouragingly. I knew there was an explanation for all of this. Peter still stood immobile. "Go on," he spat. Cold.

> Then one day, Lisa got a visit at her office here in Pembroke. She gets several visits from vendors from medical supply companies looking to partner with Pembroke, so she let the guy in. He was a short, blocky guy. He introduced himself as Matt and said he worked at Lemirk. He was also wearing a lab coat, so Lisa figured he would try to sell her some sort of insulin-injecting service for Pembroke's residents. But what he wanted was very, very different.
> Matt had been working on creating a brain neurotransmitter inhibitor using a compound

very similar to fluoxetine, which is the one used to treat depression in Prozac. But he was adapting it to help treat Alzheimer's. So he was creating a stronger, more accelerated version of it that would exponentially accelerate a patient's production of serotonin in the body to help with their cognitive brain function. Matt asked for Lisa's help to test this drug on Pembroke residents with Alzheimer's. Lisa told him that she was not the one in charge of these decisions and that he could bring it up with the community's resident doctor, but Matt insisted that it be kept between just them. And that's when he mentioned the money.

He said he'd give Lisa a thousand dollars a month while he did the tests. Then, he began speaking about how this drug could change the world and how Lisa could get a 5 percent cut on all the profits. Matt swore he was about to find the cure to Alzheimer's. And that's not even where the drug's functions stopped. He began talking about the market for regular people who could use it to simply increase their productivity. They would be millionaires, and they'd be doing a service to society.

I could see the tiniest glimmer in Lisa's eyes as she remembered the hope and excitement she felt about this at first.

"So you agreed to help him?" I nudged her on.

"Yes, I did. I knew something was not completely right. He didn't have any data to show me and he wanted to do these trials at night. And there was something just off about this Matt guy." Lisa shook her head.

"What did you do to the residents?" Peter dared to ask.

*Lisa added Matt's drug to the daily treatment of
twenty-one residents who had Alzheimer's, most of
which also lived alone. So basically no one would ask
any questions. And then, once a month, Matt would
come over at 9 p.m. and Lisa would bring the resident
to him so that he could take some quick blood and
pressure samples from them. Lisa didn't really go into
the room in the spa where he did those tests.*

"Guys, I knew something was not completely right," she
said, her voice pleading. "But nothing stood out as being
particularly wrong either. And I really needed the money.
God, I was so dumb."

There was silence in the small office for what was
probably a minute but seemed like five. I could hear the
faint hum of the air conditioning and the most imperceptible tics coming from what was probably a clock stored
in some drawer.

"Where does my dad come in?" Peter asked, his tone even
and detached.

*Matt didn't tell Lisa much about the experiments,
and she preferred it that way. A little under a year
into their arrangement, Matt called Lisa to say he'd be
holding off on the experiments for a while. When she
asked why, he said that a guy at work, Santiago, was
asking too many questions. She didn't think much of
that. But then one morning, at like 7 a.m. when Lisa
came into work early, she saw Matt sneaking out of
Pembroke wearing his lab coat and clutching his kit
under his arm. She stopped him and asked what was
going on and...*

"I can't explain to you how he was acting, but it was unsettling." Lisa shuddered.

I felt the hairs on my arms prickle at this. "What do you mean?"

"His eyes... they were all black. His pupils were completely dilated. And they were twitching. His arms and shoulders too. He was speaking so, so fast I could barely understand and he just ran away... I knew something was off with him before, but I'd never seen him like *that*. I think he started taking the pills he was testing and... I can't explain but I knew something was very wrong and I had to do something."

"Okay," Peter said impatiently, "so what did you do?"

"I have this friend who works at Lemirk, and there are surprisingly very few Santiagos who work in the labs, so I managed to find the one Matt had mentioned and I asked him to meet me for lunch."

"So he agreed, and that's why you're together in the video?" I asked, some parts of the puzzle clicking but others still missing.

"What did you speak about?" Peter added.

"He told me he had an idea of what Matt was doing. I told him he was right: something was wrong. But I warned him to stay away. I told him Matt was dangerous, and he shouldn't provoke him," Lisa said with a sigh.

"And?" Peter and I said simultaneously.

"Santiago was not having it. He said he was messaging Matt and asking him to meet us at the sketchy, horrible Burger King we were having lunch at. I begged him not to do it, but he wouldn't listen." Lisa stared off into space. "So I told him I was leaving. I didn't want to see Matt again or have anything to do with him. So I left."

There was silence again.

"So this is the day my dad goes missing and you know where he was last at and he was meeting Matt?" Peter asked slowly.

Lisa nodded.

"Then why the fuck did you not say anything about this?" Peter roared, raising his voice for the first time. There was so much anger in it you could feel it slicing the air.

"I wanted to get away so bad. Away from Matt and everything I'd done to help him. I felt like a monster," Lisa panted, more tears streaming down her face. "I didn't realize anything bad happened to Santiago until I saw the news two days after. They said he was missing. So I called Matt and all he said was… I still remember his exact words. He said: 'He was asking too many questions. And so are you right now. If you want that baby of yours to see the light of day, stay quiet and don't contact me. I'll reach out again when it's safe to carry on with the experiments.'"

I felt a cold chill run through my body.

"I…" Lisa tried to come up with words. "Peter, I'm so sorry. I wanted to do something, I really did. But Jim was in rehab and I was alone and all I had was my baby girl… I couldn't…" Lisa's voice broke again and she looked down.

"All these years, Lisa… They found his body. You knew Matt murdered him. It's been all these years and you still haven't said anything?" Peter asked, with more sadness than anger in his voice this time.

"I haven't been able to get away," Lisa said. "Matt sent me pictures of my house every other month. Didn't say anything, just sent me the picture. Threatening me to stay quiet or else… And in those two years after the, um, the incident, four residents he had been testing on died. For no apparent reason. They just died. I really didn't know what to do or who to tell.

What would I even say? I had no proof of anything and Jane was just a year and a half and…"

I shook my head in disbelief. This was horrible.

"Why was he here? About a month ago? We know Matt was here and you were with him," Peter pressed on. He was not giving Lisa any breaks, crying or not.

Lisa took a deep breath in and continued, "About a year ago, he called. He said it was time to start the trials again. I said there was no way, residents had died and this was serious… I don't think he was thinking straight anymore, but I couldn't get out of it. So I had to let him back in. But more residents he was testing on kept dying…"

"So you plan on watching them all die and letting this fucking murderer walk the streets?" Peter asked, anger creeping in again.

"What's the alternative, Peter?" Lisa asked, her voice frail. "I know the police brushed off your father's case because Lemirk red-taped it all. So who would even hear me? And what if he got to Jane before? I can't risk that."

We all sat there, again in silence.

"Here's what we'll do," Peter decided, his eyes shining intently. "You'll tell me when Matt's coming and where he goes to do his trials. Then I'll videotape him testing on the residents. With that and the conversations he had with my dad I found on his laptop, there's no denying what happened. I'll confront him about it and also try to get a confession to take to the police."

"Peter, I—" Lisa began.

"Lisa, please, I need to do this my way," Peter said calmly. "And don't worry, he'll never know we spoke or you said anything to me."

Lisa nodded somberly.

"So when is the next time he'll be coming to do the tests?" Peter asked.

Lisa looked down at her phone then back at us. "In two days."

The three of us sat there in silence. A bulky, uncomfortable silence that swallowed all the empty space in the room and choked us from the inside. I was familiar with it; the silence that hung heavy with the weight of knowing too much. Much more than any of us ever wanted.

THREAD TWENTY-SIX

———

I'm heading to Pembroke tonight, read Peter's text, the one I got as I sat on the tanning chairs by Pembroke's pool the afternoon of Matt's scheduled visit.

Ever since our conversation with Lisa, I'd been debating whether I should go with Peter to film Matt doing his tests and potentially confront him. After hearing what Lisa said, I was terrified, but I also couldn't trust Peter to keep his cool around this guy. Not after he had lost it with Lisa. This guy was dangerous. What if Peter tried to press him more than he should? I had to go.

This text was the first I'd heard from Peter after we talked to Lisa. Listening to all she said had been a lot for me. I couldn't even begin to imagine just how hard it was for him.

I'm coming with you, I texted back before I could change my mind. Then I reapplied some sunblock and flipped.

No Penelope, you really don't have to, he texted back thirty seconds after.

I know but I want to.

This might be too dangerous for you.

What do you mean for me? I texted, bouncing off the chair and starting to pace around the pool area. I had honestly been scared about going but him doubting my ability to "handle it" really made me want to go now.

I just don't want you to get hurt, he finally texted back, a full two minutes after.

I won't. We won't. We'll stay safe, I sent the three texts back to back to back before picking up my pool stuff and heading back to my apartment for a shower and some mental preparation time.

* * *

At 9:08 p.m. I found myself crouching behind some bushes in Pembroke's gardens right outside the spa's window, next to Peter. Lisa had directed us to the place and the location Matt would be at. She was standing around the spa's main entrance pacing back and forth. We'd agreed to keep her out of it for the sake of her daughter, so I made an effort to not even look her way.

Peter placed his phone strategically on the window sill before Matt walked in to set up his tiny testing station. It consisted of two of the spa's chairs facing each other. He sat on one of them and made each resident take turns sitting across from him. He pulled out tubes and instruments and note pads from his bag and used them on the residents before putting them back in. All while being recorded by Peter's phone.

In the cool night air, crouching next to Peter, I felt like things might be all right. Feeling the heat of his presence and hearing his jagged breathing reminded me what we were doing was bigger than us. It was bigger than him trying to get answers about his father's death. It was bigger than me trying to help him to prove something to myself. And it was bigger than both of us using the investigation to spend more time together. It was about saving people's lives.

Lisa headed back into the spa and, a few minutes later, she was walking out again, followed by Matt and the group of thirteen remaining residents. Peter and I waited until they walked off enough for them not to hear us and followed behind quietly. We had agreed to wait until Lisa and Matt split: her going to escort all the residents back to their apartments safely and him back to his car he parked by the main gate. Peter and I would follow him there and… I'm not really sure what would happen then.

* * *

Then came sooner rather than later, and suddenly Peter was power walking ahead of me to catch up with Matt.

"Hey!" Peter called out. On the dimly lit road leading to Pembroke's gate, I couldn't see much. What I did see was Matt's figure slow down, turn around slightly, and keep on walking toward the gate, but this time more quickly.

"You, yes, I'm talking to you!" Peter said, breaking into a small jog. "Wait up."

Matt did the exact opposite of that and started jogging too. My heart was already beating fast so I settled for power walking a few feet behind.

"Stop! Come on, just stop. Matt!" Peter commanded.

At the sound of his name, Matt stopped and turned to face Peter slowly. "How do you know my name?" Matt asked, and for the first time ever, I heard his voice. It was low and raspy. It almost seemed like he was hissing.

Just as he began speaking, I pressed the "record" button on my phone and held it down by my side. Just in case.

"I know what you're doing here," Peter said, catching up to him.

"Who are you?" Matt asked. As I got closer, I was able to see into his eyes. Lisa was right: they were two empty, black holes. "And who's she?" he added, pointing at me.

"You're giving the residents your drug. Eight of them have died already, but you won't stop," Peter spat, bypassing all of Matt's questions and going straight to what he wanted to say.

"How do you know—what are you talking about?" Matt asked, catching himself.

"Oh, you know exactly what I'm talking about," Peter said, lowering his voice and coming an inch too close to Matt. I was standing very close to Peter now so I couldn't see his eyes, but his voice was laden with something more than anger. Hate. "I saw what you did to them and you won't be getting away this time."

"I don't know what you're talking about, man. Who the fuck are you anyway?" Matt asked again. It was then I began to notice his body twitching. A subtly increasing twitch. At first just the muscles in his thighs. Then his shoulders and the fingers on his hands.

"You want to know who I am? I'll fucking tell you who I am! I am Peter. Nadler. The son of the man you murdered."

Peter's words hung in the night air for a while, dripping venom. The venom he'd held inside all these years wondering: *Who? What? Why?* He finally knew and was spitting it all out.

"I—you're crazy. I don't know who you are. I don't care. Just get the fuck away from me," Matt stammered. His words were all strung together, and he was out of breath. His head had begun twitching as well.

"Matt, there's no use in denying it," I piped in. It felt weird to hear my own voice, so soft and quiet it almost got lost in the night.

It was also my voice that apparently set Matt off.

"Who the fuck is she? What the fuck, man, I'm so confused. I did nothing to Santiago. And there's nothing wrong with the trials. I literally only take a blood and pressure sample," Matt began, his eyes, legs, and arms twitching incessantly. "It's good for them," he went on. "The pills are good for them. And for us. They can save us all. They can help us. Lisa's the one who dealt with Santiago. I told her to just let it be but she wouldn't listen." With this, his whole body began shaking and I thought he was going to have a seizure, but he kept going. "They're not just stopping Alzheimer's. They can make us all superhumans. Like superheroes almost. Who the fuck are you though?"

Peter and I stood in silent shock at what seemed like a manic episode. This guy could not stop twitching. He was completely unhinged. Everything about him was wrong. And I couldn't even begin to process what he'd said about Lisa... it couldn't be. It had to be him.

"It was Lisa?" Peter's words seemed to echo in the night air, bouncing off its emptiness.

"I told her someone was asking questions," Matt said, his twitching oddly under control for a minute. "She said I had to take care of it but I... Kill? No, no. Not me." He began pacing a little, shaking his head determinately from side to side.

"Why would I believe you?" Peter asked, with exasperation in his voice. He'd had it.

"She texted me to come help her clean up. Said if I didn't she'd tell what I was doing and they'd *destroy* my pill. I couldn't let her."

"Let me see." Peter extended his hand expectantly.

"I'm not giving you my phone," Matt said, taking a step back and clutching his phone in his left hand.

"Show me then," Peter ordered, moving a step closer again.

"Back off, man. I told you the truth, just let me be. Who is she either way?" Matt asked, his black pupils aimed at me.

Peter took a deep breath, and I thought I could discern a smile overtaking his lips. "You know who she is, Matt? She's the one who will help me get you into jail. You're done here."

"No," Matt said, his whole body suddenly still. "No, no, no. No." He began pacing back and forth. "I told you it was Lisa."

"About my dad, maybe. But those trials you're doing? They're illegal," Peter said calmly. I couldn't tell what he was going for, but I really hoped it worked.

"I'm too close. I can't be stopped. No. Not now. You have nothing. No proof," Matt hissed, shaking his head violently, clenching and unclenching his right hand into tight fists, his phone still in his left one.

A drop of blood fell from Matt's hand onto the gray asphalt. Presumably from him having dug his nails so deeply into it. This guy was absolutely losing it.

"Oh, Matt," Peter began, but in one swift movement, Matt brought his blood-stained hand to Peter's throat. I gasped, my feet frozen in place with horror. But in that split second, I also saw an opening: Matt's phone fell from his hand to the ground.

"You want to kill me, huh?" Peter asked, his lips still parted in a smile. "Or will you wait for Lisa to do the dirty deed and just help her clean up?" He was face to face with the man who had begun the chain of events leading to his dad's murder, but he had the upper hand now, and he wanted Matt to know that.

"Shut up," Matt said, his outstretched arm twitching.

He was still holding Peter by the throat and didn't seem to have realized his phone fell from his other hand. It was now or never. I knelt and quickly scooped up his phone, without either of them noticing.

"I can shut up. But that doesn't change the fact we've got—"

"Nothing," I said, interrupting him. I knew Peter wanted to see the defeat in Matt's eyes when he told him about all the proof we had recorded. I knew he almost needed that. But I couldn't let him. Matt was quite literally out of his mind. And he was holding him by the fucking throat.

"What?" Matt asked, letting Peter go.

"Yes, Matt. We have nothing. But we thought we could talk to you and make you see—"

"No. No. I don't want to talk. I don't want to see. Leave me alone," Matt said and broke into a run toward his car.

To my relief, Peter didn't run after him. We stood there, silent except for our agitated panting in the black of the night; the moon's beams reflecting off the ruby red smears on Peter's throat.

THREAD TWENTY-SEVEN

———

I don't think I really remember the days that followed. They were a whirlwind of calling the police that very same night after confronting Matt. Of having them look through Matt's unlocked phone and finding the conversation with Lisa that proved she had done the deed and he was an accomplice. Of spending the night at the police station with Peter, catching Juliana up over the phone about everything that had happened while Peter demanded to be heard by the police. And heard he was. Matt was brought in for questioning within two hours. Lisa was in there by the third. Samples were being taken and proof was being analyzed.

When she walked past me in handcuffs, Lisa and I made eye contact for the briefest second. I thought I saw the tiniest glint of remorse in her perfect blue eyes. She had been so upset about Annie's death, I knew there had to be some good in her. But no amount of remorse could ever make up for what she did.

The next day I spent sleeping for the most part. Peter was busy running around making sure the investigation was on its way and giving the police all the evidence he had collected from Santiago's hard disk.

The day after, Peter texted me he was in the area to pick up some papers and offered to take me out to lunch. I had to pass. I was exhausted. And I had no clue where Peter and I stood. So much had happened, and now I had done everything I could for the investigation, I had to ask myself what I'd been avoiding: what's next?

I was done collecting information for my story on Luciano, which was the reason I'd come down to Florida in the first place. I had also helped Juliana and Peter find an answer to the most painful question in their lives, which was the other thing that had kept me down in Florida for a little longer. The hurricane had died down once it hit the coast, so I was free to leave Pembroke whenever. I'd soon have to go back up to New York to work on the edits and make sure everything was on track for my article to be released next month in April. Go back to New York. That's what was next.

Walking through Pembroke's beautiful gardens and hearing the trickle of its majestic fountains, it suddenly hit me. There was one more thing I had to do before I would feel ready to go back to New York.

* * *

That next Sunday afternoon, I went to the beach. I wore a long flowy dress that came down to just right above my ankles and I tied my hair back in a braid. Although the hurricane warning had cleared, the wind still carried an ominous chill. The sky, however, was completely clear, not a single cloud in sight. It was like a sea of all-consuming bright blue that could swallow you whole. I stood on the surface of a lone, flat rock, letting the wind play with my dress and cradle my thoughts. It was almost weird, the concept of just letting myself exist. I stood there for a while without looking at my phone, without worrying about the work I had to do on Monday or the flight I had to catch.

Sometime after, I had no idea exactly how long it was, I saw three figures coming toward me from Pembroke's gate. Juliana, Luciano, and Peter, I presumed. I'd asked them to meet me here to say goodbye.

"Hi, Penelope." Peter smiled as they all approached. It had been a week since we turned Matt into the police, and I had only seen Peter once or twice to help him gather up and present the evidence we had. I hadn't really seen Luciano or Juliana much either. I felt a weight come off me after turning Lisa in, which propelled me to get busy with writing and do my job right. Plus, I decided to do some arts and crafts.

I hopped off my rock and fished for something in my purse. "I have something for you all," I announced, pulling out three embroidered circles I had stitched, one for each.

What I needed to do before going away was to give the three of them a gift. It felt weird to just pack up and leave after they had meant so much to me these past few weeks. So I ordered a stitching kit from Amazon and managed to create three circles, each with an uncomfortably un-proportional yellow flower stitched into the middle of it. Then, because there was no way I could master stitching words, I wrote the phrase: *Keep spinning* and signed *Love, Penelope* across the circles with a black Sharpie. Definitely not the most beautiful gift, but I figured they'd appreciate it.

"Just a little something to say how much you've meant to me," I explained, as I handed a stitched circle to each.

"This is... thank you." Luciano was the first to speak. He was clearly not impressed by my artistic abilities, but he still managed to smile and give my arm a squeeze.

"This is so thoughtful of you, Penelope, thanks." Peter went next, offering one of his beautiful smiles.

"It's beautiful," Juliana said, coming in for a hug. "I thought you'd forgotten how to stich. I taught you so long ago," she added, her breath warm against my neck.

"Um, you never really taught me..."

"What? Of course, I did, silly." Juliana grinned, tilting her head to the side. She really hadn't taught me, ever.

"Are you going to forget I taught you how to paint?" Luciano teased.

"How could I?" I joked back, deciding to let Juliana's slip go.

We stood there for a while, letting the waves lick the tips of our toes and letting our thoughts sway in their crashing roar.

"Let's walk a little," Peter said to me. Then, "Wait for us here," to Juliana and Luciano.

They were both so entranced by the waves they barely nodded.

I felt my heart begin to race as we walked off.

"So when's your flight?" Peter asked.

"Tomorrow morning." I bit my bottom lip anxiously. I still hadn't finished packing.

"I have some news," he announced.

"What's that?" I asked, feeling my face heat up. We hadn't been alone for more than ten minutes since we'd been dealing with the case, and suddenly that all felt very far away.

"You know how I came down here to find answers for my dad?"

I nodded.

"Well, I did. We did. I have the answers now. And of course, I love being around Grandma here. But I'm ready to go back to my life."

"What do you mean?" I looked down at the imprints our feet were leaving on the wet sand. His larger and deeper, mine smaller and less pronounced, but both still lingering on the sand sometime after we walked away.

"My New York life."

"Oh, wow." I opened my eyes widely in surprise. I had not expected this when I prepared to say a semi-permanent goodbye to both him and Juliana. Immediately, I felt a smile starting to spread across my lips.

"I want to wait a month or so for the case to get started and make sure everything's set for me moving back there. But I guess this goodbye won't be goodbye for long," Peter explained, putting an arm around my shoulders to give them a playful squeeze.

I couldn't stop myself from smiling. Nothing was really permanent. I was on my OPT work permission period in the US, and I had no clue where I'd be—physically or mentally—in a year. But in this moment, learning both Peter and I would be up in New York for at least a few months was all I had to hear.

"That's amazing," was all I could think to say at the moment. "I'll see you soon then."

"I'm really excited. For New York and seeing my friends." For the first time since I met him, there was a lightness to Peter. He was finally free. "And for you," he added timidly.

All I gave him was a smile. *I am too.*

"We should head back," I said instead. "I want to say goodbye to the others and go finish my packing."

"Yes, of course," Peter agreed, and we spun around and begun our way back. The waves had erased most of our footsteps, but you could still see some slight dents on the sand.

"I guess this is it," I announced when we got back to Luciano and Juliana.

"Thanks for all your help, Luciano. The article will be amazing," I declared, going in for a hug.

"Do pass it along when it's done, please," Luciano replied, hugging me back.

"And thank you so much for all the stories, Juliana," I said, turning to face her.

"Of course, my dear," she cooed. "But don't leave just yet."

"I... I'll come visit. I'll call you," I offered, but I felt my throat begin to knot up.

Juliana nodded and then gave me a warm hug.

I began to walk away but stopped and turned around at the sound of Juliana's voice.

"Wait, Caroline," she called after me. "One last kiss."

"Grandma, Aunt Caroline's..." Peter began.

I shook my head at Peter to get him to stop. *Let it be, it's okay,* I mouthed.

"Remember to call when you land," Juliana said, standing on her tiptoes and kissing my cheek softly.

I nodded, not trusting myself to speak at the risk of my voice cracking. Peter looked at Juliana, as if willing her to retract what she'd said and laugh at her confusion.

She didn't.

I finally turned and began walking away. I felt a tear roll down my cheek and saw it splash down on the sand.

In the end, it didn't matter if I was Caroline or Penelope, because all great stories are about love; about feeling love. If the feeling is there, the threads can keep on spinning and there's a story. Nothing else really matters.

ACKNOWLEDGMENTS

It's been a life-long dream of mine to write and publish a book, and it's almost unreal to think I did so before turning twenty-five! However, I never knew how much work this process truly entailed and how much support you need to get through it. To those who've been there for me and supported me throughout the journey of writing and preparing to publish *Spinning Threads*--you've been instrumental in making my dream come true!

First and foremost, I want to thank my family for giving me the inspiration, motivation, and drive to write this book. To my mom and my dad, thanks for fostering the love for learning and reading in me since I was young. It is this love that drove me to treasure stories and aspire to write one of my own. To my sister, thanks for always pushing me in the right direction and being my brainstorming rock; you helped me materialize the idea for this book, and for that, I'm extremely grateful. To my grandma, thanks for all the countless stories you've shared with us throughout the years and for inspiring us with them. To my grandpa, thanks for showing us everything's possible, you just have to start small and stay true to who you are.

I also want to thank my friends for checking in throughout the process, for being my sounding board when I was unsure of where to go, and for always believing in me—you know who you are and how much you've meant to me through this adventure.

To my teachers, from my second-grade teacher Macha to my high school and college English Professors, thanks for instilling in me the passion for the art of reading and writing. There's nothing more satisfying than musing over a thought we discussed in class for hours and hours; it makes you realize how powerful stories are, and it made me want to write one.

To my editors (Elia, Mozelle, and Gina), thank you so much for guiding me through the daunting journey of writing my first full novel and helping me make it something I'm extremely proud of.

To the team at New Degree Press (namely Eric and Brian), I can't thank you enough for bringing me into this journey and having been with me throughout it. If it hadn't been for your continued support and guidance, I wouldn't have made it this far.

Finally, to all of the friends, family, and colleagues who contributed to my pre-sale campaign efforts, I'm so thankful for your support at such a critical stage in my journey. I'll be forever grateful for your incredible words of encouragement and your help:

Cristina Escalante	Antonio Vicent Fanconi
Cristina Dobles	Wesley Longhofer
Sylvia Echeverria	Libby Egnor
Carolina Escalante	Adriana Ochoa
Salud Criado Sanchez	Carlos Abarca

Gemma Harris

The Hatchery

Nicole Santolalla

Kevin Kirsch

Benjamin Tenzer

Arnav Agarwal

Julia Tisheh

Rachel Klein

Daniel Madrigal

George Harris

Zahir Palanpur

Jessica Wu

Nicole Martin

Kay Allen

Bria Goeller

Susan Klopper

Mauricio Vargas

Maria Paula Calderon Acon

Andrea Hershatter

Christine Cho

Quinn Evangelakos

Aagam Vakil

Carl Xi

Kristi Huang

Ryan McCann

Shoham Berkowitz

Christina Wi

Kathryn Butts

Sophia Heredia

Eric Koester

Liese Nainiger

Anna Gibbons

Catalina Murguia

Luis Felipe Dobles Junqueira

Jim Morey

Avery Scope Crafts

Danielle Moron

fernandezlaignel

Lynda Hu

Eduardo Chamberlain

Raul Saco

Felipe Matamoros

Devon Sullivan

Edward Lauw

Marijose Rodriguez

Adriana Calderon Acon

Patti Sullivan

Toko Miller

Mauricio Campos

Brendyn Melugin

Mary Cate Sullivan

Isabel Fernandez

Alice Yoon

Kristian Dudchak

Juan Pablo Sabillon

Carla Rodriguez

Charlotte Keeley

Maria Jose Suarez

Kenji Goto

Sylvia Araya

Akshatha Achar

Kenneth Murillo

Alejandro Dobles

Nicole Aubert

Joseph Oh

Maximilian Helmut
Fickenwirth

Ariela Farchi

Ana Cristina Perez

Keegan McCombie

Maria Thompson

Mary Elaine Hanna

Pranjli Pandya

Catalina Constenla

Michelle Soto

Devin Gu

Jeffrey Chu

Mahad Khan

Alifya Valiji

Irene Dobles

Antonio Chan

Shreya Mohan

Jasmine Zhu

Poome Thavornvanit

Kevin Seo

Naam Srisaard

Jeffrey Huai

Madhumitha Kumar

Valeria Kopper

Anne Pizzini

Lizzie Goodrich

Giovanna Herrera

Sandra Mora

Mary Elizabeth White

Sinthya Solera Ramos

Luis Felipe Dobles Junqueira

Maria Dobles

Pedro Dobles

Jessica Wu

Danielle Moron

Randall Gazel

Gabriela Dobles

Silvia Rodriguez

Antonio Bruna

Mónica González

Norman Gutiérrez

María Fernanda González Miranda

Yeeun Lee

María Concepción Sanchez Hurtado

Javier Monge Herrera

Monica Alfaro Escalante

Sylvia Escalante Vargas

Camila Font

Lucia Ruiz

Cori Arndt

Carolina Chen

Karla Polini

Deanna Altomara

Alexandra Arroyo

Marco Andrés Guirola Barrientos

Alberto Alfaro

Sylvia Ugalde

Timothy Chee Cheng Lui

Made in the USA
Columbia, SC
12 May 2021

37797756R10124